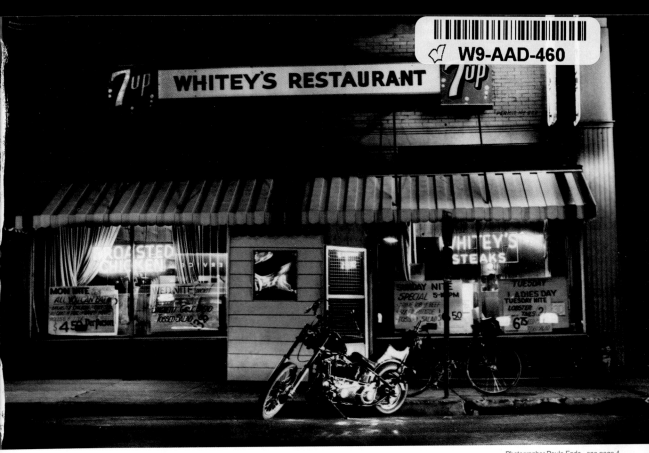

Photographer Paula Endo - see page 4

We are
ARLINGTON

Hope you like my book !

Bill Hamrock

Hamrock (H) Publishing

October 2014

To buy books in quantity or for promotional
or corporate use please email Bill Hamrock
WeareArlington@gmail.com or call 301-335-2156

Published by Hamrock Publishing Inc.
hamrockpublishing.com
4133 Maple Avenue, Fairfax, V.A. 22032
Copyright 2014, Bill Hamrock
ISBN: 978-1-4951-1114-3
Printed in the U.S.A.

Designed & Printed by KOREAMonitor®
7203 Poplar St., Annandale, VA 22003
T : 703-750-9111
www.koreamonitor.net

ACKNOWLEDGEMENTS

To my family: My wife Susie and kids Kyle, Kelly and Katie. Thanks for being special.

Helene and Liam Ebrill - Thanks for your help, support and friendship

Ken Danforth

Virginia and Jim Palmer

Judy Knudsen, Heather Crocetto and all the staff in the Arlington County Public Library System especially in the Center for Local History

Library of Congress

Arlington Historical Society

Bob Tramonte

Steve Caruthers

George Dodge

James Vandeputte

Buck and Associates Real Estate

Adele Soule

Greg and Suzanne Embree

Greg Cahill

Bill Vogelson

David Senty

Gail Baker

Susan and Henry Cassidy

Special Thank You to all who donated to the Arlington Historical Society and the Center for Local History at the Arlington County Public Library. Thank You for making history accessible.

Thank You to all the great customers of Pasha Café who admired my walls of Arlington's historic photos showing a real sense of pride and interest. This convinced me to publish this book.

We are
ARLINGTON

INTRODUCTION

Arlington, Virginia! What a great place to live, work, and have fun. A metropolitan city with small town neighborhoods. People from Arlington love Arlington. But, Arlington is much more than just its residents and businesses today. It has a rich history. That includes Arlington House-Arlington National Cemetery and its four million visitors a year, the Civil War, the Pentagon, and Captain John Smith sailing down the Potomac. The Wright brothers made history flying at Fort Myer. The transition to the community Arlington is today is a story worth telling. Many of Arlington's businesses are unique and help make the community. With its close proximity to Washington, D.C., and being home to Arlington Cemetery, the Pentagon and other memorials, Arlington gets national and sometimes world-wide attention.

The story of Arlington is not new. It is history. I have used many available references while researching this book, especially the resources offered by the Arlington County Public Library and its Center For Local History. A complete bibliography is located in the back of the book. Along with the text, the photos and images help communicate Arlington's history as well as show the current Arlington today. The pictures tell a story. For purposes of this book, I have considered present day Arlington County to be Arlington, although Arlington was part of Alexandria until 1920; prior to that it was part of Washington D.C. and before that part of Fairfax County.

I have plans to publish a volume II version of "We are Arlington." Many stories and parts of Arlington's history were not included in this book. There is much more to tell. If you have any stories, photographs, or history you would like to include, please contact me. I am particularly interested in information and photos about Arlington's small businesses.

ARLINGTON NATIONAL CEMETERY

It would not be fitting to start off a book about Arlington, Virginia, with anything except Arlington National Cemetery. Arlington National Cemetery is a national landmark. A world landmark. A final resting place for many American heroes. Many died in the name of duty, to protect the American way, democracy and those in need of help. Some died in tragic accidents testing science and engineering to make the world a better place. Some died by terrorist attacks without warning or preparation. All left behind mothers, fathers, wives, children, brothers, sisters, other family members, friends and fellow soldiers dying to protect each other and our freedom. Although I speak of Arlington National Cemetery only with great honor and respect, nothing in writing could tell the whole story. There are more than 400,000 American heroes resting here and each one has a story to tell. Stories of freedom, hope and faith. Stories of families. Stories of sadness, happiness and death. Stories of courage. The story of America. Each one is greatly missed and probably each wished their own life story had more to tell.

God Bless America and God Bless Arlington National Cemetery.

Arlington National Cemetery became a national cemetery of the United States in 1864. Originally 200 acres, the cemetery now covers 624 acres. Casualties from every major war in American history are buried here. During a tour of Arlington cemetery President Kennedy was reported to have said, *"This is so beautiful. When I die I'd like to be buried here or in a place as beautiful as this."* Unfortunately for our 35th President this came prematurely and he is buried within 100 yards of where he made this statement.

" Let Every Nation Know

Whether it wishes us well or ill

That we shall pay any price

Bear any burden

Meet any hardship

Support any friend

Oppose any foe

To assure the survival and the success of liberty "

John F. Kennedy

Unfortunately, Freedom is Not Free

A young Veteran pays his respects at Arlington National Cemetery.

*LOC

Knudsen, Robert G. *A Living Treasure-Seasonal Photographs of Arlington National Cemetery.* Potomac Books, Inc.: 2008

The Story of Arlington House

The Arlington House is in Arlington National Cemetery. George Washington's stepson, George Washington Parke Custis, inherited the land from his natural father, John Parke Custis who had purchased the property to create a plantation. G.W.P. Custis decided to create a national memorial for Washington and began building a home on the West bank of the Potomac River in 1802. It became "Arlington House."

In 1831 the daughter of G.W.P. Custis, Mary Ann Randolph Custis, married a young Army lieutenant named Robert E. Lee. The couple eventually took over responsibility for the house and day to day plantation operations. The Lees departed Arlington House as the Civil War commenced and Lee took command of the Confederate Army. Arlington House then became a headquarters for the Union Troops. It became government property after the Lees were unable to pay a property tax that had to be paid in person in Washington, D.C. As the war continued, the Union Army's Quartermaster General Montgomery Meigs was tasked with surveying locations for a cemetery. It was Meigs who changed Arlington House from a memorial to President George Washington to a military graveyard. The location was chosen with greatful disregard for Confederate General Robert E. Lee and to meet the need for a burial ground.

The Decision

Lee's Decision to join the Confederate Army was not an easy one. He had high ranking offers from both sides. He was a West Point graduate. Lee had already achieved a highly distinguished and respected career of more than thirty years serving his country. Most of his colleagues and friends would be on the side of the Union. Although his home was in Arlington, Virginia, it was only a stone's throw from Washington, D.C. Lee's wife was in poor health. Uprooting her and the family would cause tremendous pain. They also had no set plan as where they would go and live. In the end it came down to this *"All the Lees had been Americans,"* wrote Douglas Southhall Freeman, Lee's biographer, *"but they had been Virginians first."*

The decision was made with great pain. Lee's sister lived in Baltimore and was married into a Union family. Her son was a Union captain who would soon be at war. Lee's three sons would also serve in the war. His decision would have an effect on them. Here are the words from a letter Lee wrote to his sister, hoping for her understanding as their own family was forced to choose sides in a conflict that would scar the nation forever.

> *With all my devotion to the Union, and the feeling of loyalty and duty of any American Citizen, I have not been able to make my mind to raise my hand against my relatives, my children, and my home. I have, therefore, resigned my commission in the Army and save in the defense of my native state (with sincere hope that my poor services may never be needed) I hope I may never be called upon to draw my sword.*
>
> *I know you will blame me, but you must think as kindly as you can, and believe that I have endeavored to do what I thought right. To show you the feeling and struggle it has cost me I send you a copy of my letter of resignation. I have no time for more. May God guard and protect you and yours and shower upon everlasting blessings, is the prayer of*
> **Your Devoted Brother R. E. Lee**

On April 23, 1861, Lee accepted command of Virginia's military and naval forces, with the rank of Major General. From that moment Lee's home in Arlington was lost and chances are that Lee knew it.

Union Soldiers at Arlington House June 28th, 1864.

It became a nostalgic photo for Union soldiers to have their pictures taken in front of the home of the now Confederate General, Robert E. Lee.

*LOC

Poole, Robert M. *On Hallowed Ground-The Story of Arlington National Cemetery.* Walker & Company: 2009

Montgomery C. Meigs

Quartermaster General Montgomery C. Meigs was a Georgian who remained loyal to the union. He disliked the Confederacy and those serving in it. In his mind they were traitors. Meigs found himself responsible for the dead soldiers ending up in Washington. Mortuaries were opening up all around the city next to houses, markets and restaurants. *The Washington Chronicle* reported and complained *"it insults the meanest animals to have their dead and food in juxtaposition."* There seemed to be a never-ending flow of bodies. Meigs petitioned Secretary of War Edwin M. Stanton for permission to turn the Arlington House and surrounding property into a military cemetery. Without waiting for formal authorization, internment began on May 13, 1864. Formal approval came one month later. In October of 1864 Meigs' own son, Lt. John Rodgers Meigs, chief engineer of the Army of the Shenandoah, was gunned down by Confederate cavalry men and was buried at Arlington National Cemetery. The hatred was now joined by personal grief.

Meigs and Lee were both career military. Both were respected and capable in their fields. For 30 years they had been on the same side. Now, this was a nation at war, brother against brother causing great pain. These feelings continued long after the Civil War ended. The Confederates felt that Arlington was a Union Cemetery and part of the Union wanted to keep it that way. The approval and unveiling of the Confederate Monument with its great symbolism, almost 50 years later, helped ease the pain for many.

" Not for Fame or Reward
Not for Place or Rank
Not Lured by Ambition
Or Goaded by Necessity
But In Simple
Obedience to Duty
As They Understood It
These Men Suffered All
Sacrificed All
Dared All and Died "

Engraving on the
Confederate Monument

Confederate Monument

Veterans in uniform leaving the Confederate Monument.

A celebration ceremony at the Confederate Monument June 4, 1914.

Meigs Strikes Again

In an August 1864 visit to Arlington, Quartermaster General Montgomery C. Meigs was furious to find the graves had been dug a half mile away from the mansion. *"It had been my intention to have begun the internments nearer to the mansion,"* Meigs had noted. He then supervised the next 26 bodies to be buried along the perimeter of Mary Custis Lee's beloved rose garden. Meigs later ordered the Unknown Civil War Solders Tomb to be placed in the center of the rose garden.

Unknown Civil War Solders Tomb (2013).

* LOC

Group visiting the Unknown Civil War Solders Tomb (early 1900's).

Unable to return to Arlington, Robert E. Lee and Mary Custis Lee spent their remaining years on the campus of Washington College (today known as Washington & Lee University), in Lexington, Virginia, where Robert E. Lee died on October 12, 1870. He is not buried on the grounds of his former home, but is interred in the chapel on the campus that now keeps his name. Lee's son George Washington Custis Lee eventually won a settlement from the U.S. government over property rights to the family's land, it was theirs once again. Since the property now had more than 17,000 graves on it, they agreed on a monetary settlement and the property remained in the hands of the government.

Time and History

Time and history are what have made Arlington National Cemetery such a sacred world landmark. Its origins were to be a military cemetery. A place the dead were buried when they couldn't be returned home. A cemetery meant to make the Arlington House uninhabitable by the Lee Family.

On May 30, 1868, President Andrew Johnson gave all Federal workers the day off for the first "Decoration Day" now known as Memorial Day. By the end of the 19th century, Arlington National Cemetery had almost 19,000 graves with an average of one interment per day. War dead from the Revolutionary War and the War of 1812 were reinterred here to extend the cemetery's historical era. The mass burial, with over 20,000 in attendance, of sailors of the USS Maine raised national awareness of Arlington National Cemetery. The burial of prominent Civil War heroes, including Major General Philip H. Sheridan in 1888, elevated Arlington's status. Two World Wars and the Korean War increased its size. The death and burial of President John F. Kennedy is what made the cemetery such a landmark. The President's burial was seen by a worldwide television audience. Within three years, 16 million visitors made a visit to the site. Requests for burials in Arlington dramatically increased. A demand aggravated by the 56,000 American deaths during the Vietnam War, resulted in as many as 47 funerals a day. Newer eligibility rules have sharply restricted burials. Space is the challenge to the cemetery's future. At the current rate, the cemetery will reach capacity in 2060.

"Arlington" by Trace Adkins

In 2005 country music star Trace Adkins recorded a song titled "Arlington." The song was honoring, thankful and respectful. It was moving up and had made it to number 16 on the country music charts when Trace pulled the song from the charts. He had received complaints from families that had loved ones buried at Arlington. It was not his intention when recording the song to be offensive to anyone. This only proves how real war is and that emotions run high for families missing loved ones. Also that our freedom is not free.

"*Let us here highly resolve that these honored dead shall not have died in vain*"

Abraham Lincoln-The Gettysburg Address

These words are engraved in the amphitheater at Arlington National Cemetery.

* Photographer Greg Embree

The Tomb of the Unknown Soldier is guarded 24 hours a day, 365 days a year in any weather by Tomb Guard sentinels who are also known as the Honor Guard. January 30, 2010. The temperature this day was 16 degrees with a wind chill of 7 degrees.

* Photographer Greg Embree

The changing of the guard occurs every 30 minutes in the summer and every 60 minutes during the winter months.

Monuments and Memorials

There are many monuments and memorials throughout the cemetery. Historic and respectful, they honor many of America's most courageous men and women.

The Battle of Meuse-Argonne

The battle that ended World War I but also cost the lives of 26,277 Americans.

The Pearl Harbor Memorial

Remembers the attack on Pearl Harbor, Dec 7, 1941, which brought the United States into World War II.

The second Schweinfurt Raid Memorial

Honoring the American airmen who fought German fighters during a World War II raid on the town.

The Battle of the Bulge Memorial

Remembers the courageous stand Americans made against the attacking German Army from Dec 16, 1944, to January 25, 1945, in Belgium and Luxemburg. *The greatest land battle in the history of the US Army.*

The Khe Sanh Memorial

Remembers the Marine base that withstood a siege lasting over four months in Vietnam.

Argonne Cross

"In memory of our men in France 1917-1918."

Beirut Barracks

In memory of the 241 American servicemen who were killed in the bombing of the American barracks in Beirut, Lebanon on October 23, 1983.

Tomb of the Unknowns (also known as the Tomb of the Unknown Soldier)

"Here rests in honored glory an American Soldier known but to God"

Canadian Cross of Sacrifice

A memorial to honor the large number of United States citizens who enlisted in the Canadian Armed forces and lost their lives during WWII. As Canada entered the war before the United States, many Americans enlisted in Canada to join the fighting in Europe. Few countries share the friendship and goodwill that the US and Canada have. The border between The U.S. and Canada is the longest unguarded frontier on earth.

Coast Guard Memorial

Honoring those in the Coast Guard which was formed as the successor to the Revenue Cutter Service and The Life Saving Service June 28, 1915.

Iran Rescue Mission

"In Honor of Members of the United States Armed Forces who Died During an Attempt to Rescue American Hostages Held in Iran 25 April 1980."

Korean War Contemplative Bench

"In Sacred memory of those Americans who gave their lives during the Korean War 1950-1953"

Nurses Memorial

The large white marble figure honors the Army, Navy and Air Force Nurses who served in the U.S. armed forces during World War I.

Pan Am Flight 103 Memorial

The Lockerbie Cairn, a gift from the people of Scotland. The 270 blocks of red Scottish Sandstone, memorializes the 270 lives lost in the terrorist attack when Pan Am flight #103 was bombed Dec 21, 1988, over Lockerbie, Scotland.

President John Fitzgerald Kennedy Gravesite

On November 22, 1963, while campaigning in Dallas, Texas, President Kennedy was shot and killed while riding in his open limousine.

President William Howard Taft Monument

The 27th President of the United States from 1909-1913.

Robert F. Kennedy Gravesite

The former attorney general and Presidential Candidate was shot June 5, 1968, and died the next morning.

Rough Riders Monument

The First U.S. Volunteer Cavalry. Officially dedicated on April 12, 1907. The Rough Riders served with distinction during the Spanish American War.

Space Shuttle Challenger Memorial

Shortly after taking off on Jan 28, 1986, the Space Shuttle Challenger exploded killing all seven crew members.

Space Shuttle Columbia Memorial

Upon re-entry, after a 10 day mission, the Space Shuttle Columbia was lost on February 1, 2003 with seven crew members aboard.

Spanish American War Monument

"To The Glory Of God And In Grateful Remembrance Of The Men and Women Of the Armed Forces Who In This Century Gave Their Lives For Our Country That Freedom Might Live"

The USS Serpens Monument

The largest single disaster suffered by the United States Coast Guard in World War II happened on the night of January 29, 1945. Two hundred and fifty men died.

The USS Maine Memorial

The original main mast of the USS Maine, which was blown up and sunk in Havana, Cuba, February 15, 1898.

Foreign Nationals

Throughout history the United States has counted on friends and allies around the world for support. Some of those individuals who helped our country in times of need were given special rights at Arlington National Cemetery. Altogether 64 foreign nationals lay at rest inside the cemetery grounds. Twenty-four are British. Other countries represented are: Australia, Canada, China, Holland, France, Germany, Greece, Italy, Iraq, South Africa, and Vietnam.

Arlington National Cemetery

The Image: To be the best. Perfection. America's premier military cemetery. A national landmark and shrine. To honor America's heroes with respect and dignity. Honoring the history of America's freedom and democracy that lives on today.

For the most part, eligibility for interment into Arlington National Cemetery is reserved for active duty or retired members of the U.S. Armed Forces. High ranking government officials and individuals who lost their lives due to terrorism or hostile force by foreign government or agents are also included. Special exceptions can also be made.

Here is a short glimpse of 11 Americans Interred at Arlington National Cemetery

William Henry Christman: The first soldier interred in the cemetery. William was a twenty year old farm laborer who enlisted into the 67th Pennsylvania Infantry on March 25, 1864. On May 1, 1864, he was diagnosed with measles and died less than two weeks later on May 11.

William Blatt: A 19 year old from of Berks County, Pennsylvania, William enrolled in the 49th Pennsylvania Infantry on September 1, 1861. On May 10, 1864, William received a gunshot wound to the head at the battle of Spotsylvania, Virginia and died shortly after. William was the third soldier buried in the cemetery and the first battle casualty of war.

Wiley Neal: A 23 year old from Jeffersonville, Virginia, Wiley was killed by an artillery shell in the Argonne Forest, France, in the last week of WWI.

Robert Scott: A 26 year old native of Maslin, Ohio, Robert attended Ohio State University. He died in the attack on Pearl Harbor.

Henry Elrod: From Rebecca, Georgia, Henry attended college at Georgia and Yale Universities before he enlisted in the US Marine Corps in 1927. At Wake Island on December 9 and 12, 1941, pilot Elrod shot down two planes and sank the Japanese destroyer Kisargi. This was the first major warship sunk by a fighter plane carrying only small caliber bombs.

James Johnson: From Pocatello, Idaho, James was killed in combat at Yudanini, Korea, on Dec. 2, 1950. The platoon leader and World War II veteran was last seen *"in a wounded condition single handedly engaging enemy troop in close hand to hand grenade and hand to hand fighting/combat."*

Vincent Doyle: Grew up in Locust Gap, Pennsylvania. Graduated from West Catholic High School in Philadelphia and Villanova University. Served in the army during the Korean War. While teaching at Vare Junior High School in South Philadelphia he met his future wife Clare McNierney. They eventually settled in McLean, Virginia, where they raised six children and are responsible for 13 grandchildren. Vince was a proud Fourth Degree Member of the Arlington, Virginia branch of the Knights of Columbus. He was also always willing to help at St. Luke's Catholic School and Church in McLean, Virginia. St. Patrick's Day was one of his favorite days and he loved backyard family cookouts.

John F. Kennedy: Our nation's 35th President, JFK was a Medal of Honor recipient for his service during World

War II. On November 22, 1963, Kennedy was shot and killed in Dallas, Texas, while traveling in an open limousine with his motorcade. Initial reports that Kennedy would be buried near his home in Brookline, Massachusetts, were corrected when First Lady Jacqueline Kennedy declared the President *"Belonged to the people"* and should be buried at Arlington National Cemetery.

Ed Burke: Attended Manhattan College on an ROTC scholarship and was active military (Air Force) for 27 years. His last assignment as a Colonel was working for the Joint Chiefs of Staff at the Pentagon. During college Ed sold beer at Yankee Stadium where mastered the sales pitch, "cold beer here," "cold beer here" for life. He was a lifelong Yankee fan. He married Mary Murphy and they had four girls together which turned into 11 grandchildren. Ed was a proud member of the Newport Rhode Island Ancient Order of Hibernians. Easter morning flowers for his girls were one of his favorite rituals.

Glenn Miller Memorial: The Big Band leader, composer and trombonist. During World War II Glenn Miller's Army & Air Force band entertained more than a million troops. Major Miller combined military and musical precision to create a band which many say was even better than his civilian band. Too old to be drafted, Miller volunteered his services. On Dec. 15, 1944, he took off on a flight from London, England to Paris, France. The plane never reached France and was never found.

Joe Louis: "The Brown Bomber" held the title of heavyweight champion of the world longer and defended it more times than any other boxer in history. As a Sergeant during World War II, he donated $100,000 to Army and Navy relief efforts and fought 96 exhibition matches for more than two million troops.

A view of the Washington Monument (under repair) from Arlington National Cemetery (2013).

Grave Markers

Throughout the rolling hills and fields of the cemetery most of the grave stones are very similar and simple with little engraving. They are part of the solemn beauty of Arlington National Cemetery. There was a time when families were allowed to create their own headstones. Some are quite elaborate. Here are 18 examples of gravestones at Arlington National Cemetery.

JOHN
MAXWELL
DICKEY Jr
DISTRICT OF
COLUMBIA
1ST LT
US AIR FORCE
JUL 20 1939
MAR 25 1965

51 543

FOR GOD AND HIS COUNTRY
HE RAISED OUR FLAG IN
BATTLE AND SHOWED A
MEASURE OF HIS PRIDE AT
A PLACE CALLED IWO JIMA
WHERE COURAGE NEVER DIED

THOMAS JOHN KILCLINE SR.
VICE ADMIRAL
UNITED STATES NAVY
DECEMBER 9, 1925 ——— JULY 11, 2002
WIFE, MOTHER, GRANDMOTHER
DORNELL THOMPSON KILCLINE
FOUNDER, NAVY ARLINGTON LADIES
NOVEMBER 8, 1926 ——— MARCH 6, 2007
BELOVED SON
PATRICK JOSEPH KILCLINE
LIEUTENANT (JUNIOR GRADE)
UNITED STATES NAVY
LOST AT SEA IN AN F-14
APRIL 21, 1953 ——— JULY 16, 1978
BELOVED DAUGHTER
KATHLEEN MARIE KILCLINE
LIEUTENANT, MEDICAL CORPS
UNITED STATES NAVAL RESERVE
AUGUST 26, 1955 ——— OCTOBER 16, 1980

TIL WE MEET A

VINCENT
JOSEPH
DOYLE
CPL   USA
1930   1994

HOYT

JAMES McCUBBIN LINGAN
an officer of the Maryland line in the
War of the American Revolution

A captive on the Prison Ship JERSEY

An original member of the
Society of the Cincinnati

Born May 13, 1751 · Died July 28, 1812
and his beloved wife
JANET HENDERSON
Born Sept. 2, 1765 · Died July 5, 1832

Honor to their ashes
Peace to their souls

"Hallowed Ground"

A place so special and significant words could never describe its true meaning. There is no place more inspiring. No place more humbling. A place of great history with sacrifice and unanswered questions. It is relaxing and peaceful. Powerful with honor and pride. A final resting place for many American heroes who died to protect our freedom.

> " *I am not a soldier or even a writer. I don't feel worthy to write about Arlington National Cemetery. But I am an American and Damn Proud of it.* "

Bill Hamrock

This is Arlington

29

CIVIL WAR
The Arlington Line

No place was disrupted more than Arlington (still part of Alexandria at the time) during the Civil War. It became the Union Army's. They took what they wanted. Since Virginia was enemy territory, there was no concern for the property they were disturbing. Property was destroyed, farm crops and animals confiscated and roads built through the middle of farms. For the entire war, Arlington was occupied by Union troops. The occupation of 10,000 Union troops overwhelmed the population of 1,400 men, women and children. The simple farming community was changed forever.

The Union troops occupied Arlington to protect the nation's Capital. They built a series of 23 forts throughout Arlington known as "The Arlington Line." Although a large part of the Civil War was fought in Virginia, and the nation's Capital seemed a likely target, the defenses in Arlington were never directly attacked by Confederate Armies. It is safe to say the Arlington Line served its purpose.

Five years after the war, Arlington was nowhere close to recovery from the effects of occupation by Union troops. The withdrawal of the Union Army was quick, but a large mess was left behind by their defenses. Almost every tree in Arlington was cut down, either for fuel or visibility (to see a clear line of fire). It took until almost the turn of the century for the farms in Arlington to flourish again.

* LOC

Fort CF Smith was built in early 1863 near Spout Run. Company F, 2nd New York Artillery, Fort CF Smith, August 1865.

* LOC

The back gate at Fort Corcoran. Fort Corcoran was one of Arlington's earliest forts built in May, 1861
to help control access to the Aqueduct Bridge near the site of today's Key Bridge.

* LOC

Gun crew of Company K, 2nd New York Artillery, Fort C.F. Smith, August, 1865.

* LOC

1rst Connecticut Artillery at Fort Richardson. Fort Richardson is now home to the Army-Navy Country Club.

* LOC

Training at Fort Whipple, which was built in early 1863. Fort Whipple was maintained as a permanent military post and the name was changed to Fort Myer in 1880.

* LOC

The big gun at Fort Corcoran. Soldiers of the New York 4th Artillery, 1862.

* LOC

The big gun at Fort Woodbury. Fort Woodbury was located very near the present day courthouse and built in August 1861. It was named for Major D.P. Woodbury, the engineer who designed and constructed the Arlington Line.

* LOC

Colonel William H. Telford and officers, 50th regiment Pennsylvania infantry at Fort Craig.
Fort Craig was constructed in August 1861, located on the present day South Courthouse Road at South 4th Street.

* LOC

Chain bridge under guard during the civil war. The Union army feared the Confederate forces would try to capture the bridge for its easy access to Washington, so Fort Marcy and Fort Ethan Allen were built for protection.

*LOC

Union Soldiers on the Arlington side of the Potomac River.
The Aquaduct Bridge and Georgetown University are in the background.

*LOC

The 107th U.S. Colored Infantry at Fort Corcoran.

* LOC

Officers of the 69th New York Militia, Fort Corcoran.

* LOC

Officers of Company K and L, 2nd New York Heavy Artillery, at Fort C.F. Smith, August, 1865.

Freedman's Village

During the Civil War freed slaves made their way into Northern Virginia and Washington D.C. to find a safe place and a new beginning. Most arrived with little or no clothing or other possessions. They had limited skills and there were few jobs for them. Overcrowding, hunger, crime and disease spread rapidly. In 1863 the Federal government established Freedman's Village as a place for them to live and gain skills. Freedman's Village was located on the Eastern edge of Arlington Cemetery. The village consisted of 100 framed houses and provided shelter, clothing, food, medical care, schools and training in employable skills. The Freedman earned $10 dollars a month in wages. The intent was not to provide permanent housing, but a temporary residence to learn a skill and find employment. Once a job was found freedmen were encouraged to move out and make room for others. Abolitionist and preacher Sojourner Truth lived at Freedman's Village for about a year, counseling residents and finding work for the unemployed. The village closed in 1888. Queen City was formed near here by decedents of Freedman's Village but was eventually razed in order to build the Pentagon. The city was not on the Pentagon building site but was lost to accommodate parking and surrounding roads for the project.

Freedman's Village, drawing May 7th, 1864.

* LOC

THE PENTAGON

The largest direct impact on Arlington was the building of the Pentagon. The population of Arlington doubled in three years and nearly tripled in ten as people moved to the area to work for the federal government. The Pentagon was designed and built at record pace. Contracts for its construction were finalized on Sept. 11, 1941, and ground was broken the same day. A limited amount of steel was used in the design of the building due to short supply from its use in World War II. No marble was used because Italy, the largest supplier of marble, was an enemy of the United States at the time. Instead, the Pentagon was built with concrete, using 680,000 tons of sand dredged from the Potomac River. A lagoon was created beneath the Pentagon's river entrance. More than 41,000 concrete piles were sunk into the swampy site to stabilize the foundation. Thirteen thousand workers worked around the clock and completed construction in just sixteen months. For much of the time, concrete was being poured 24 hours a day. After the attack at Pearl Harbor on Dec 7, 1941 there was additional pressure to speed up the design and building. At times the construction was moving faster than the design. The Pentagon was built one wing at a time. When one wing was completed employees would move in while construction continued on to other wings. The United States Postal Service established six zip codes for the building. It has been said that there are more than 100,000 miles of telephone cables in the walls and floors of the Pentagon.

* ACPL-CFLH

The early days of the Pentagon. Employees have already moved into some parts of the building while it is still being constructed.

The Pentagon is one of the world's largest office buildings, containing more than 6.5 million square feet of space. Inside, no two offices are more than 1,800 feet apart, about a six and a half minute walk. To walk completely around the outside of the building would be almost a mile. At the time of its heaviest use during World War II, 37,000 employees worked in the Pentagon. The number today stands closer to 25,000. The building covers 34 acres and has 17 and one half miles of corridors.

The Pentagon was constructed when racial segregation was enforced. Because of this, separate eating and bathroom accommodations were constructed for black and white employees. These displays of segregation were done in compliance with the Commonwealth of Virginia's racial laws. As a result, the Pentagon has double the number of toilet facilities needed for a building of its size. On President Franklin D. Roosevelt's initial tour of the Pentagon he put a stop to racial discrimination in the building. For a long time, the Pentagon was the only building in Virginia where racial segregation laws were not enforced.

Looking across the Potomac River into Washington D.C. An old Pentagon postcard, 1950's.

Originally the Pentagon was known as the War Department Building. At the time of its construction, in 1941-1943, no one knew the significance the Pentagon would have for the U.S. military, intelligence and its place as a world landmark. Most everyone believed the Pentagon was a temporary solution due to World War II. After World War II the world was a different place. There were constant threats from around the world against the U.S. and its allies. A larger military force was maintained, nearly eight times the size it had been prior to 1940.

* ACPL-CFLH US Army Public Domain

An artist's drawing for a building design that was being considered for the Pentagon.

The March on the Pentagon

Because of its great importance and military stature, the Pentagon sometimes becomes the focus of protests and national events. One of the largest is known as the "March on the Pentagon." On October 21, 1967, the National Mobilization Committee to End the War in Vietnam, a loose association of protest groups, sponsored and organized the largest antiwar rally in American History. It received official sanction for the rally for a forty eight hour period over the weekend of October 21 and October 22. The rally began at the Lincoln Memorial and then marched on to the Pentagon. An estimated 35,000 people assembled at the Pentagon. They were met by more than 2,000 armed soldiers, police, guardsman, helicopters, tanks and other military support. Other military units, including 2,500 men from the 82nd Airborne Division were held in reserve at Andrews Air Force Base, Fort Meade, Fort Myer and Fort Belvoir. Late in the afternoon on Saturday, October 21, about 2,000 protesters broke through the lines and attempted to enter the Pentagon but were turned away by additional troops inside the building. Others began to throw rocks and bottles at the troops and building. The soldiers pushed the crowds back, and strong reactions on both sides led to injuries. By that night the majority of the crowd had dispersed and a smaller, quieter demonstration followed on Sunday.

The Pentagon Fire

One of the fiercest and most intense fires to test the ability and coordination of the Arlington County Fire Department was the fire at the Pentagon on July 2, 1959. The fire started in a computer room operated by an Air Force Agency and burned for more than five hours. There was no sprinkler system. The fire was deep inside the Pentagon. The firefighters' air tanks were used up trying to get to the fire and out of the building which left them less than 10 minutes at a time to fight the actual fire. A book published in 1976 by the National Fire Protection Association listed the Pentagon fire among the nation's worst. Although there were some close calls, and more than 30 firefighters were sent to local hospitals, nobody died in the fire. In all, 300 firefighters and more than 70 units responded.

September 11, 2001

A day no one will ever forget. On the Pentagon's 60th anniversary of its groundbreaking, terrorists crashed American Airlines Flight 77 into the Pentagon at 9:37 a.m. All 53 passengers, 5 hijackers and 6 crew members were killed, as well as 125 people in the building.

The area hit was under renovation. Only eight hundred of the usual 4,500 people were in this part of the building. This section of the building was best prepared for an attack. Because of the 1995 bombing in Oklahoma City it had been reconstructed with steel columns and bars to withstand bomb blasts. The steel reinforcements kept that section of the building from collapsing for 30 minutes, enough time for hundreds of people to crawl out to safety. It was the only part of the building with a sprinkler system. The area also had blast-resistant windows that stayed intact after the crash and fire. It also had newly equipped fire doors that opened automatically and newly built exits that allowed many people to escape.

* Photographer Greg Embree

September 11, 2001 Memorial at the Pentagon.

Arlington County Fire Department

Responds to the Pentagon September 11, 2001

There was almost no time to react. The Boeing 757 was headed straight for the Pentagon. The screaming engines were racing over 500 miles per hour lining up for a direct impact. The plane had taken off from Dulles Airport, just miles away with full fuel tanks ready for a coast to coast flight. The plane skimmed the ground and slammed into the western side of the Pentagon. There was a terrible roar, an explosion and a blast of heat. Flames were raging on all five floors of the Pentagon. The heat was incredibly intense, melting steel. Concrete floors caved in, pancaked. Thick black smoke turned the morning light into the darkest night.

The jet fuel burned violently. It was impossible to reach the center of the fire. The concrete building and slate roof made it difficult for the firefighters. Precious time was lost because special tools and equipment were needed to cut through the building. There were several times throughout the day when firefighters were ordered to evacuate the building, fearful of another attack or building collapse. Firefighters dealt with flames and hotspots for the next two days. The fire wasn't declared under control until 3pm on September 13th. The recovery effort intensified. Search and Rescue teams were arriving from across the country. At 7a.m. on Friday, September 21st, the recovery effort officially ended and the site was declared a crime scene, with the Federal Bureau of Investigation taking over from the Arlington County Fire Department.

Almost 3,000 people died in New York City at the Twin Towers site, including 343 members of the New York City fire department. At the Pentagon 189 people died. Although there were injuries, there were no deaths in the Arlington County Fire Department. Another plane, United Airlines Flight 93, crashed in rural Pennsylvania as passengers heroically struggled with hijackers. Another 44 people died there. That plane was likely headed towards Washington, D.C. In all, the death toll on September 11th topped Pearl Harbor. Nineteen fanatics, trained and supported by Osama Bin Laden, had committed mass murder. Arlington was a major part of Tuesday, Sept. 11th, 2001. The day that changed our country. After the twin towers fell, the Pentagon reclaimed the title of *"The World's largest office building."*

Vinny Del Giudice, *'The Red Book' - A Century of Service*. Second Edition 2002

AIRPORTS

Arlington was once home to two airports. Hoover Airport opened in 1926 and was Arlington's first airport. A year later Washington Airport opened on a nearby site. Within a few years the two airports combined their operations. The two airports were located where the present Reagan National Airport is located and part of the area which is now the Pentagon. Air traffic in the area had several unique challenges since part of the old Military Road crossed through the airport grounds and was used for automobile traffic. In 1938 President Roosevelt directed that a new and larger airport be built, and in 1941 Washington National Airport was opened for operations alongside the Potomac River. It was renamed Ronald Reagan Washington National Airport in 1998.

Washington Airport (1930's).

* ACPL-CFLH

View from the airfield (1930's)

View from the airfield (2012)

Main entrance to Washington National Airport (mid 1940's)

* ACPL-CFLH

Main entrance to Ronald Reagan National Airport (2014)

Air Travel

Flight records were established by Orville Wright and his brother Wilbur in the early 1900's at Fort Myers. Orville Wright began testing the flying machine Wilbur had invented. On September 12, 1908 he stayed in the air for one hour and 15 minutes. The next year Orville completed the first cross country flight by airplane. The advancement did not come easily. On September 17, 1908, Orville Wright crash landed on the Fort Myers field, killing passenger Lt. Thomas Selbridge, who became the first victim of an airplane crash. Orville also received injuries from which he never fully recovered.

*LOC

* LOC

Practice flights at Fort Myer, 1906 and 1909.

1909 flight at Fort Myer

* LOC

* LOC

September 17, 1908 Wright's plane crash-landed at Fort Myer killing passenger Lt. Thomas Selbridge.
The cause of the crash was a broken propeller.

The first air passenger service to New York began in 1928.

Plane taking off, 1930's.

* ACPL-CFLH

Updating the flight schedule the old fashioned way!!
August 1942-National Airport.

*LOC

Eastern Airlines young essay winners 1938, Washington Airport.

*LOC

A few years later. Eastern Airlines, Great Silver Fleet, at Washington National Airport.

A busy place. Planes landing and taking off, 2013, Reagan National Airport.
The Wilson bridge is in the background.

Just after take-off, 2013 Reagan National Airport from Gravelly Point, just across the runway.

US Space Shuttle Discovery
April 17th, 2012

* Dasha Rosato/Shutterstock.com

A curtain call for the space shuttle Discovery on its way to retirement.
One last ride around the DC Metro area included Arlington and a fly-by at the Pentagon.

Three airplane accidents involving the Arlington County Fire Department (ACFD).

June 6th, 1928- A monoplane on a test flight from Hoover Airfield went into a tailspin over Arlington Beach and crashed into the Government's Experimental Farm (now the land is part of the Pentagon or Arlington Cemetery). The ACFD sent two trucks. Both men on board the plane died, one at the scene and the second on the way to the hospital.

November 1, 1949- A Bolivian Air Force Fighter, just purchased from the US Government, was on a practice run and slammed into Eastern Airlines flight 537 as it approached National Airport. All fifty five passengers and the crew died. The ACFD spent thirty hours at the scene until all victims were found. The tail of the airliner just missed the Mount Vernon Memorial Highway near Four Mile Run. At the time, it was considered the deadliest civilian aircraft accident in the country.

January 13, 1982- Air Florida flight 90, carrying eighty three passengers and crew, came out of the swirling snow to hit one of the bridge spans on the 14th street bridge. The plane sheared through five cars, ripped through fifty yards of guard rail and plunged nose first into the icy Potomac River.

Just after four p.m. the Arlington County Emergency Communications Center received a telephone call from CB operator Evie White, advising of trouble on the bridge, possibly an aircraft down. Before cell phones that's what the ACFD had to go with, "We didn't know what we had," said Captain Howard Piansky, *"We thought it was a small plane."*

What they had was much worse. Of the eighty three people on board only a few survived the initial crash into the freezing Potomac River. They were struggling in the cold water with ice chunks, debris and jet fuel. On the bridge, four people were dead while others were injured and trapped in their crushed vehicles. The US Park Police helicopter, Eagle One, arrived to assist in the rescue. Hovering over the river, Eagle One plucked four people to safety. One crash survivor, Arland Williams, vanished in the river after passing the helicopter lifeline on to others. An autopsy showed that Williams was the only victim to drown.

Federal employee Lenny Skutnick, who was on his way home from the Congressional Budget Office, jumped into the river to help rescue a woman who was too weak to make it to shore after falling short on the helicopter rescue line. D.C. firefighter John Leck also went into the water to help.

Vinny Del Giudice, *'The Red Book' - A Century of Service.* Second Edition 2002.

IT'S ALL FUN AND GAMES

Arlington Beach

Swimming in the Potomac was a popular pastime in the 1920's. Arlington Beach was an amusement park located at the south end of what is now known as the 14th Street Bridge. The beach opened on Memorial Day in 1923 to a crowd of 7,000 and flourished until the end of the decade. Canoeing, swimming, rides and games were featured. It also had a ferris wheel, roller coaster, merry-go-round and dancing. The beach closed in 1929 and was demolished with the expansion of the airport. Almost all swimming ended in the Potomac with the construction of the George Washington Memorial Parkway in the 1930's.

* ACPL-CFLH

A day at the beach.

*LOC

A bear of a day June 27, 1924.
Renee Dixon and Bess Baker taking "Ted" for a swim at Arlington Beach. Ted was raised by Miss Baker since he was a tiny cub and enjoyed his daily swims on hot summer days.

Fun and Games on the Water

* LOC

The 14ᵗʰ Street Bridge is now located almost exactly where this picture was taken.

* LOC

Canoeing continues to be a popular pasttime on the Potomac today.

*LOC

A Motley Crew!! Enjoying a day at the beach.

*LOC

Fun and games? Maybe not so much!

* LOC

* LOC

Local beauties posing for a picture. Washington Monument in the background.

Luna Park

Luna Park was an elaborate amusement park built in 1906 on 40 acres at Four Mile Run on the line of the Washington, Alexandria and Mt. Vernon Railway. Huge buildings in various architectural styles (Gothic, Moorish and Japanese) were built. There was a large ballroom, circus area and restaurant. A merry-go-round, carnival rides and other attractions were also there for fun and entertainment. Unfortunately, the fun did not last long. The exact date the park closed is not known, but by 1915 it was being dismantled. The site remained stagnant for decades. The Arlington County Sewage Treatment Center now covers the site.

SHOOT THE SHUTES, WASHINGTON LUNA PARK.

"Shoot the Chutes" water ride.

Luna Park was described by its promoters as a "fairyland of amusement overlooking the beautiful Potomac."
It claimed to have room for 3,000 picnickers.

A special attraction for the park was three elephants, which arrived in a boxcar from Coney Island.
Their first performance was a crowd pleaser. That night a violent thunderstorm came through and the elephants broke free and
were on the run. A few days later they were found some sixteen miles away in Burke.

Winners of the Arlington five mile, 1922. An automobile racetrack was located in Jackson City. Jackson City was a notorious area that had become an embarrassment and danger to the County. It was known for its saloons, gambling rooms and brothels. Crandal Mackey, the Commonwealth Attorney, helped lead the way for cleanup of the area in 1903. The Pentagon would later take the land that was Jackson City.

Local boy scouts in a fire-starting competition (around 1910).

July Fourth Parade at Fort Myer (1940).

* ACPL-CFLH

Youth sports and activities are a big part of the Arlington community. Go Blazers.

* ACPL-CFLH

Washington-Lee, High School State Champs (1931).

Boys will be Boys

The Arlington Duel

In 1826, very close to the current Chain Bridge, a duel took place between Secretary of State Henry Clay and United States Senator John Randolph of Roanoke. Before the Senate on March 30, 1826, Senator Randolph made comments that were taken as an insult by Clay. Secretary of State Clay called Senator Randolph out for a duel. General Jessup, who was to be one of Clay's seconds delivered the challenge to Randolph. Efforts made by friends to smooth out the differences were futile, and arrangements were made for the duel.

Saturday April 8th, 1826, at four thirty in the afternoon was the time set. A spot in a dense forest just above the Little Falls Bridge, as the bridge was then named, was the place. Pistols were the weapons. The distance was ten paces and each party was to have two seconds and a surgeon. There was to be no practicing. General Jessup and Senator Josiah S. Johnston of Louisiana were Clay's seconds. Colonel Tattnal, a congressman from Georgia, and General James Hamilton of South Carolina were the seconds for Randolph.

The night before the duel, Mr. Randolph went to see General Hamilton and told him that he would receive Clay's fire but not return fire. "Nothing shall induce me to harm a hair of his head, I will not make his wife a widow, or his children orphans." Randolph's friends tried to convince him to change his mind but their attempts were rejected. Randolph did remark *"If I see the devil in Clay's eye and that with malice prepense he means to make my life, I may change my mind."*

At the appointed time and place, the principals saluted each other courteously, as they took their places on an east and west line. As they took their positions, Randolph's pistol went off with the muzzle down before the order was given. Colonel Jessup, Clay's second, called out that he would leave immediately with Clay if this happened again. But Clay with noble generosity asserted that it was clearly an accident. Another pistol was handed to Randolph and the duel was on. An exchange of shots followed. Randolph's bullet struck a stump behind Clay, and Clay's knocked up the earth and gravel behind Randolph.

The pistols were reloaded, and Clay's shot knocked up the gravel behind Randolph, as his first shot had done. Randolph raised his pistol and fired in the air, and exclaimed, *"I do not fire at you, Mr. Clay,"* and advanced his hand to Clay. Clay met him half way and the two shook hands Randolph whose coat skirt had been pierced by Clay's bullet near the hip, replied, *"You owe me a coat, Mr. Clay,"* and Clay replied promptly, *"I am glad the debt is no greater."*

Ruth M. Ward, *A Duel in Arlington - Arlington Historical Society Magazine*, 1981.

Bernie's Pony Ring

Every summer in the early and mid 1950's a little amusement park came to Lyon Village (now the home to the Italian Store, Giant and CVS). There were several rides for small children, and the pony ring was the main attraction. The ponies were kept *"in the country"* in Merrifield.

* Photo compliments of Adele Soule

Adele Kirby Soule's 6th Birthday Party, July 20th, 1958.

* Photo compliments of Adele Soule

Adele's favorite pony was named "Peanuts."
Photos taken by Elgin Kirby, owner of Kirby's Corner and later Kirby's Dodge.

Percy Walton, Karl Kight, Harvey T. Knight Jr. and Harry Davies at the Washington Canoe Club (1921).
Karl and Harvey Knight competed in the 1924 Olympic Games. They have medals to prove it.

Working out on the Potomac River. A daily ritual for many.

Local colleges and high schools can be seen training their crew teams on the river almost daily.

Enjoying the Potomac River

Crossed Sabres

Vol. 23, No. 5   WASHINGTON—LEE HIGH SCHOOL, ARLINGTON, VIRGINIA Wed., Nov. 24, 1954

W-L, GW To Clash In Traditional Thanksgiving Game; 10,000 Fans Anticipated At Alexandria Stadium

Ten thousand fans, not bad for a high school football game.

OFFICIAL
PROGRAM
10c

GEO. WASHINGTON HIGH SCHOOL
vs
WASH.-LEE HIGH SCHOOL
THURS., NOVEMBER 22, 1956 - 11:00

The old *"Oaken Bucket Game."* An annual game played on Thanksgiving morning between Washington-Lee of Arlington and George Washington from Alexandria.

Tom Calhoun   Jerry Whitehouse   Jerry Meroney

Jerry Hite   Art Eberdt   Tom Beauford

Jim Palmer   Paul Cundiff   Warren Beatty   Bill Swift   Ed Brown

Washington-Lee seniors (1954).

* Compliments of Virginia Palmer

Advertisement from the 1956 game day program between Washington-Lee and George Washington.

High school gym class at Washington-Lee, 1950's.

* Photographer Paula Endo - see page 4

The Marine Corps Marathon is an annual tradition that started in 1976. With a field of 30,000 runners the starting line is located between Arlington Cemetery and the Pentagon. The finish line is located just beyond the Marine Corps Memorial. The Marine Corps is currently the third largest marathon in the country and eighth largest in the world. The 26.2 miles starts in Arlington, continues into Georgetown, Washington D.C. and then finishes back in Arlington.

Capital bikeshare is a bicycle sharing system located throughout Arlington and the metro area.
This promotes a healthier lifestyle, easy access and eases transportation.

Arlington Parks and Recreation does a great job throughout the County. Although much of Arlington is very much a city, there are all types of parks, fields, bike paths, streams, hiking trails, frisbee golf, tennis courts and more available for exercise and enjoyment throughout the county.

Washington Golf and Country Club

The Washington Golf and Country Club was organized as the Washington Golf Club in February, 1894, by a group of members of the Metropolitan Club of Washington. Originally the club's nine hole course was located in Rosslyn. In 1908, the club moved to its current location on North Glebe Road when it bought 74 acres from Admiral Rixey. In the early years it was known as the club of presidents. Presidents Taft, Coolidge, Hardy and Wilson were all active members. A few years after buying the land from Rixey the club realized it needed more land from him. Board member Dr. Johnson proposed that he and Admiral Rixey play a round of golf for the plot. If the Admiral lost, he would give the club its needed land, if he won the club would pay for it. Dr. Johnson won the match and the Admiral was as good as his word. Another forty seven acres, the Grunwell tract, was added in 1919. The club is in its second century as a leader, the first golf club in Virginia and the ninth club to join the USGA.

* Compliments of Steve Caruthers

David Bates, Steve Caruthers, President George H. W. Bush and Dorrance Smith.
The foursome played dozens of doubles matches together while the President was in office. Most were played at the White House but several matches were played at Washington Golf and Country Club. This picture is taken after one of those matches. The play on the court was very competitive and the outcome was almost always a very close match.

Army Navy Country Club

Established in 1924, Army Navy Country Club sits on the old Fort Richardson site, which was part of the Arlington Line during the Civil War. Past members have included General Omar Bradley, Presidents Eisenhower, Kennedy, Johnson, Nixon and Clinton.

Kettler
Capitals Iceplex

The official home of the Washington Capitals. Capitals practices are held here and are free to the public. Kettler also offers public skating, figure skating, and hockey programs for youths and adults year round. Kettler Capitals Iceplex is a state of the art facility located at the top of the Ballston Common Mall parking garage. In addition to the 20,000 square feet training center for the Capitals, the Iceplex features two indoor NHL sized rinks, office space, locker rooms, a full service pro shop, a Capitals team store, a snack bar and place for special events. The Capitals majority owner-chaiman and CEO of Monumental Sports and Entertainment is Ted Leonsis. He is also a graduate and supporter of Georgetown University. Leonsis takes a hands-on approach to managing his sports teams and is an active leader in the community.

ARLINGTON IN TRANSITION

Arlington was originally *"the country part of Alexandria County,"* rural farmland. During the Civil War, Arlington was one big defensive fortification, run by the Union Army to protect the Nation's Capital. Post-Civil War years were not pretty, with disorder and lawlessness in parts of Arlington. Farmers and citizens were working hard to clean up their land and get back to farming. Then in the early 1900's came the extension of trolley lines and the Washington & Old Dominion Railway from Alexandria to Bluemont Virginia (a popular resort in the Blue Ridge Mountains) and from Georgetown to Great Falls. This expansion led to neighborhoods such as Bon Air, Lyon Village, Clarendon, Ballston, Cherrydale, Maywood and Glen Carlyn. These settlements were full of civic enterprise, energy and community spirit. Full of life, the new Arlingtonians were doers, expecting nothing from Alexandria County. They developed their own schools, libraries and community centers. Growth started to take off in the early part of the turn of the century.

In 1920, to avoid confusion between Alexandria County and the city of Alexandria, the name of the country part of Alexandria County was changed to Arlington. The name was derived from the Arlington Estate and to honor Robert E. Lee. By the late 1920's and 30's Arlington was expanding rapidly. During World War II, with the building of the Pentagon, Arlington's population doubled and the infrastructure began to meet the needs of a metropolitan area.

* ACPL-CFLH

A couple of early Arlingtonians
Mary Ann Hall

Arlington's Madam

In the 1800's a number of prominent Washingtonians purchased farmland in Arlington (still part of Alexandria County at the time) and used it as country retreats and summer homes. Mary Ann Hall was one of those people. She bought a total of 80 acres. She was a special lady, very attractive as well as a prostitute and was known as a keen business person. She owned an upscale brothel at the foot of the U.S. Capitol for more than 40 years until her death in 1886.

After her death, Mary Ann Hall's farm was bought by Admiral Rixey. The farm later became Washington Golf and Country Club and Marymount University. "Mary Hall's Spring" survived on the golf course, near the 14th green, until it was demolished in 1959.

Bazil Hall "Hall's Hill"

Mary Ann Hall's Notorious Brother

In 1850 Bazil Hall purchased a 327 acre farm that would today be located just west of the North Glebe Road and Lee Highway intersection. Although he was likely born in Washington, Bazil spent time as a whaler in Massachusetts, in South America and in California, where he met his first wife. Bazil was a character remembered for his bad habits, violent temper and his poor treatment of everyone, including his slaves. On one occasion they attempted to burn his house down. On December 14, 1857, Bazil's first wife, Elizabeth, was brutally murdered by one of their slaves. The property and family suffered the worst of hardships during the Civil War. The family's house and barn were burned by Confederate troops who claimed it was being used by Union troops to spy upon rebel lines. Soon after, Union troops occupied Hall's Hill and cut down all the trees to get a better view towards Falls Church and Upton's Hill. Most of the land was sold to his children but some of the land in the northwest corner was sold to his ex-slaves.

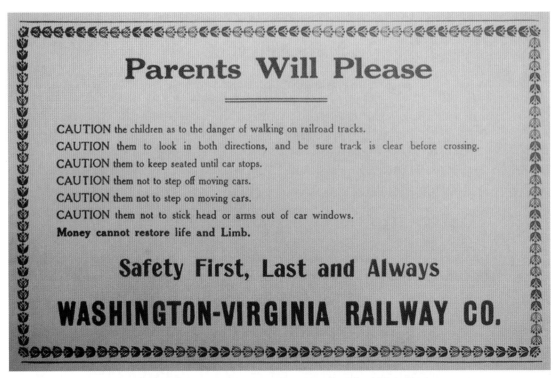

Advertisement for the Northern Virginia Exposition. Clarendon, Virginia (1915).

The U.S. Army Officers Club. Fort Myer, Virginia (early 1900's).

The brand new Arlington County Refuse Collection, (1940).

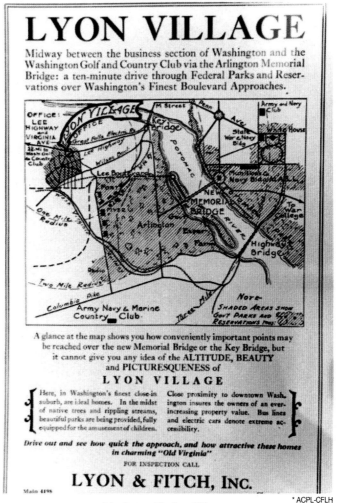

Advertisement for Lyon Village

Rosslyn

In the late 1800's and early 1900's the Rosslyn neighborhood was a rough area dominated by gambling, saloons, and brothels. One main path through Rosslyn was known as *"Dead Man's Hollow"* where a dead body was reported to be found on the average of one a week. Local farmers returning from a day of selling in Washington D.C., would set up armed conveys before returning through Rosslyn. The struggle to clean up this area was led by Frank Lyon's *"Power of the Press"* and Crandell Mackey's fearless posse.

Washington, Arlington, Ft. Myer and Falls Church Station, Rosslyn, Va.

* ACPL-CFLH

It wasn't until the 1960's and 1970's that the Rosslyn skyline really began to change. The original planning for Rosslyn came before Metro. It called for more of a building-to-building approach rather than a store front approach. Also left out originally were residential dwellings.

An aerial view of Rosslyn (around 1956).

* ACPL-CFLH

The Rosslyn Skyline (2012).

Jackson City

Crandall Mackey, the Commonwealth's Attorney, was the first to take on Jackson City, which was an unsavory area established on the south side of the Long Bridge in 1835. John Nelson was one of the last to fight Jackson City. John Nelson was a gambler. He lived the gambling lifestyle, consistently in and out of jail. One night he had some trouble in Jackson City, he wasn't treated right. He took the matter into his own hands and decided to burn the place down. With the fire still burning he made it back to Aman's Saloon and let the boys know *"look over there, she's a goner now, I fixed her this time."* Jackson City burned down and was never rebuilt.

Unfortunately for Mr. Nelson, he now had a real problem on his hands. Arson was a serious crime, with execution a possibility. John Nelson got one of the best lawyers in Northern Virginia to defend him. R.Walton Moore was his attorney who later ended up as the Assistant Secretary of State and served in Congress. At the time R.Walton Moore's argument was this, *"Gentleman of the jury, John said he didn't burn the city down, he says he didn't do it. But I want to say something about it. If he did burn it down, it is the greatest favor ever done to Arlington County by any human being."* After a five minute deliberation, John Nelson was acquitted by the jury.

Senator Frank L. Ball, *The Arlington I Have Known - The Arlington Historical Magazine*, 1964.

Clarendon

Clarendon has always been considered the center of Arlington County, downtown or the shopping district. It was one of the earliest neighborhoods in Arlington that had deliberate planning with laid out streets. The district had been thriving after the World War II boom but in the late 1950's and 1960's the area began to suffer. Businesses were moving out to newer areas such as Tyson's Corner. It wasn't until the late 1980's and well into the 1990's that Clarendon began to thrive again. The Metro worked for this neighborhood, bringing thousands through the area daily and today many businesses are thriving there. Business, office space and residential space are still growing, but it was not an overnight success.

Home Depot to Clarendon? In the 1990's the Arlington County board received a proposal from Home Depot to open a store in the center of Clarendon. The Board took its time to research the proposal and perform its due diligence, while at the same time Home Depot was making counter proposals with upgraded enhancements. A year and a half into the talks, just when it appeared the County Board was approving the proposal, Home Depot decided to pull out. The County Board received a lot of flak from some citizens for allowing this to happen. Many people thought the Board had too much power. Could you imagine a Home Depot in the Center of Clarendon now? It sure would not be the same Clarendon that we enjoy today.

Clarendon Station; This site is now the home of Northside Social.

* ACPL-CFLH

The old Ashton Theatre. Affectionately known as the "Ash Can." This site is now the home of the Clarendon Metro.

CLARENDON CITIZENS' ASSOCIATION.

This organization has been in continuous existence for about ten years. During that time it has been instrumental in securing a school for Clarendon, sidewalks, street lights, increased powers for the Board of Supervisors, permission to bond the county in the same amount as cities, and many other important matters.

Before any sidewalks were laid by the county, this Association laid over two miles of cinder walk. Before the electric and gas companies existed this Association maintained street lights in Clarendon.

The dues are nominal, being only one dollar per year. One year's dues must accompany the application for membership.

President........................R. P. Hugh
Vice President.................A. F. Snyder
Secretary......................A. L. Reinberg
Treasurer......................A. J. Porter

This Association is the owner of its home, known as the Clarendon Engine House, and in promoting the interests of Clarendon, it has afforded fine quarters for the Clarendon Board and Clarendon Athletic Association.

Every white resident of Alexandria County 19 years old, and of good moral character, is eligible for membership.

Old Advertisement for the Clarendon Ctizens Association (1915).

* ACPL-CFLH

Lee Highway (1940's)
Just beyond the Esso Station would be the entrance to the present day Lyon Village.
The bus on the top right would be the entrance to Kirkwood Street.

* ACPL-CFLH

Lee Highway looking west (approximately 1923 in Cherrydale).
This picture was taken from the roof of the Old Dominion Bank Building which is now gone.
The house on the right is at the present-day Safeway.
The trolley tracks are those of the Washington and Old Dominion Railway, Great Falls branch.
Eventually the use of the automobile reduced passenger service and put the railway into bankruptcy.
Old Dominion Drive to Great Falls was constructed following the removal of track.

Ballston

One of the first established neighborhoods in Arlington. Named after the Ball Family. One of Arlington's first prestigious shopping centers, Parkington, was built there in 1951. Parkington was later greatly upgraded into the Ballston Commons shopping mall. One by one the "Ballston Corridor" was created with the building of the Metro and the high rise office and apartment buildings that would later follow.

Glebe Road

Wilson Blvd.

* ACPL-CFLH

The very beginning of Ballston-Parkington (1951).

* ACPL-CFLH

Parkington

Then and Now, Ballston

* ACPL-CFLH

Corner of Glebe Rd and Wilson Blvd.

* Photographer Greg Embree

Shirlington

A great example of a thriving business district and neighborhood in Arlington that does not rely on Metro. Signature Theatre, the Movie Theaters and some very good restaurants keep this area thriving. Shirlington has also incorporated a County Library, grocery store and many residential units to keep the area consistently busy.

Shirlington(1959)

* ACPL-CFLH

George Washington Parkway

The parkway's original name was the Mount Vernon Memorial Parkway. As early as the 1880's plans were being made for a national road to visit George Washington's family estate at Mt. Vernon. By the 1920's, two hundred thousand people a year were visiting George Washington's family estate at Mt. Vernon. In 1929 Congress re-named it the George Washington Memorial Parkway. Portions of the parkway were considered a model of modern highway design and got special recognition.

* ACPL-CFLH

George Washington Parkway (1953). Facing NW from Rosslyn – Key Bridge.

The same shot (2013)

Two Sets of Three Sisters

Three Sisters, One: The three rocky islands in the Potomac River just west of Key bridge are known as the *"Three Sisters."* The little islands were significant landmarks in early maps of the region. Various legends are associated with them. One of the earliest myths involves three Algonquian sisters who crossed the river in an attempt to win release of their brothers, who were captured by another tribe. They drowned on the crossing and never made it.

The Three Sisters on a cold January day (2014).

Three Sisters, Two: The Navy opened Radio Arlington in 1913, located by Ft. Myer. At the time the set of three radio antennas were the world's tallest. They were similar in construction to the Eiffel Tower. One of the Towers was 45 feet taller than the Washington monument. The first trans-atlantic voice communication was made between this station and the Eiffel Tower in Paris, France in 1915. The nation set its clocks by the Arlington Radio time signal and listened for its broadcast weather reports. The time signals also helped ships at sea calibrate their navigational equipment. The three towers were dismantled in 1941 as a menace to aircraft approaching the new Washington National Airport.

*ACPL-CFLH

Sears Homes in Arlington

Imagine picking up your new home at the train station. Between 1908 and 1940, Sears Modern Homes were built and sold by mail order. Over that time, Sears offered 447 different home styles for sale, including the Arlington (Model #145). The exact number is not known, but it is reported that 100,000 of these homes were sold. Many of these homes are still standing, surviving all different types of weather throughout the country and additions to their original appearance. This proves the quality of craftsmanship. Arlington was a perfect market for the Sears Modern Home.

When the Great Depression hit, it was Sears liberal loan policies that eventually doomed Sears Modern Homes. 1929 saw the high point, with sales more than $12 million, but almost 50% of that was in mortgage loans. In 1934, $11 million in mortgages were liquidated, dooming the Sears Modern Homes Program. By 1935, Sears was no longer offering financing and sold its last house in 1940.

Sears was not the only one to have *"Kit Houses"* in Arlington and outside; Montgomery Ward, Aladdin Homes and Rucker's Lumber based in Rosslyn were competitors. It is estimated that there were over 1,000 Kit Houses built in Arlington.

* Photographer Greg Embree

A Sears House still standing in North Arlington. This is the Conway Model built around 1923 for Samuel Vanderslice and his family. Vanderslice was the first Principal at Washington-Lee High School.

Knights of Columbus

The Edward Douglass White Council of the Knights of Columbus, located in Arlington, Virginia, was founded in 1923. Today this branch of the Knights of Columbus is thriving, with close to 1,500 members. It offers its venue and services to the membership and the general public. The Columbus Club (sister organization to the Arlington Knights of Columbus) was honored by Arlington County and the Arlington Chamber of Commerce by being named Arlington's Best Business in the category of Service Small Business of the Year. The Arlington Knights of Columbus uses the former home of George Saegmuller, his wife and in-laws the Vandenbergs. The home was known as Reserve Hill.

George Saegmuller was a well known and distinguished Arlington resident. He was a native of Germany and came to the United States at the age of 23. He is known for helping develop Arlington. He advanced funds for a new school in 1890. He was very influential in locating the County Courthouse in 1898. He was also chairman of the County Board of Supervisors. He achieved success as an inventor and manufacturer of scientific instruments. He was the holder of 41 patents used by the military and in the optical profession. When the original house burned down in 1892, Saegmuller built a stone mansion to replace it. A desire to have running water, the first in Arlington, led him to build the water tower. The shape of the tower came from the image on a beer stein depicting the Nuremburg, Germany, city wall that Saegmuller gave to the stone mason as a model for the tower. The first private phone line in the County was installed in 1894 to run between Reserve Hill and Easter Spring Farm, on North Glebe Road, the home of Saegmuller's brother in-law.

The Greatest Scandal in Arlington History

E. Wade Ball had been elected County treasurer in 1907 and was re-elected six times. In his last election in November 1931 he was not challenged. The Ball family was a well-known family in Arlington. *"Ballston"* bears the family name.

E. Wade Ball was sentenced to two and one-half years in the state penitentiary for failing to turn over $515,969 in County funds. The missing funds in terms of today's budget would be equivalent to approximately $460,000,000!!! Hard to miss that kind of money and very strange he was given such a lenient sentence.

During the trial two Georgetown banks testified that Ball had deposited $26,000 and $47,000 annually for a period of 7 years. Those deposits would have totaled $511,000. The withdrawal and allocation of the funds and its recipients were never disclosed.

Candidate for Re-election to the Office of County Treasurer

E. WADE BALL

An advertisement by E.WadeBall (1915)

"Where did the money go?"

That is still the big question. Was there some sort of conspiracy to protect prominent citizens and businesses who may have been beneficiaries? Some suggest that we look no further than the 15 citizens who testified on Ball's behalf. Others have suggested that E. Wade was a latter day Robin Hood doling out the County's money to those in need. E. Wade was a simple man. He was not a big spender or a flashy dresser. When his assets were seized they were very modest and he was left penniless. After serving his two and one half years E. Wade went to work for Lyon Realty. Thereafter he is referred to as *"realtor."* The *"Great Scandal"* was seemingly over and not discussed.

The reason for E. Wade's downfall was the newly-formed Arlington County government. In 1931 the first five member County Board was elected and its first order of business was to appoint Roy S. Braden as County Manager. It was on Braden's first day as County Manager that he recommended an audit of the Treasurer's Office. Could it have been that the acts of the Treasurer had been widely known among Arlington's leading citizens? Ironically, E. Wade's brother and attorney, Senator Frank Ball was a major architect in the design of the new government.

Ken McFarline Smith, a distinguished Arlington attorney and author of "Bar Nostalgia-Memories and Reflections of the Arlington Legal Community," noted that he detected a conspiracy of silence. *"Unless I missed a source, everyone clammed up, most were adults in 1932 and they carried their "knowledge to their graves."* There was a brief mention of the scandal in the *"Memoirs of Tom Phillips."* He stated that *"the details are not important here."*

Right or wrong, the details were important at one time. That kind of money had to have had a major effect on the county and to the people that knew about it. Maybe it was the best way to handle the scandal. Maybe it wasn't a scandal at all. We will never know. It's history now.

Frank O'Leary, *The Greatest Scandal in Arlington History... The Saga of E. Wade Ball.* Article found in the Center for Local History at the Arlington County Public Library.

The Rixey Mansion

Rixey's former home is now the site of the Washington Golf and Country Club, Marymount University and St. Mary's Episcopal Church.

Rear Admiral Presley Marion Rixey was born in Culpepper, Virginia, in 1852. In 1873, after nine months of study, he received his medical degree from the University of Virginia. Rixey served in the Navy in Europe and the South Atlantic before being assigned to Washington in 1882. While in Washington, Rixey bought the "Netherfauld Farm" located in Arlington where he later built "The Rixey Mansion."

In 1901 Rixey became the personal physician to President McKinley. He then served as President Theodore Roosevelt's personal physician. The Roosevelt family often visited Rixey at Netherfauld, where the President and Rixey would hunt and fish. Admiral Rixey retired as Surgeon General of the Navy in 1910. He volunteered to serve again during World War I and then returned to Virginia in 1918.

On the day of Admiral Rixey's death at the age of 76 in 1928, he applied the finishing touches to his autobiography. He wrote:

" *In regard to my long life, I believe I have achieved success, have lived well, laughed often and loved much; I have gained the respect of intelligent men, and the love of little children; and have filled my niche and accomplished my task. I hope I will leave the world better than I found it and that it will never be said that I have lacked appreciation of Earth's beauty or failed to express it. I have tried to look for the best in others and have given the best I had.* "

Chain Bridge

* ACPL-CFLH

Chain Bridge during the flood of 1937.
The original bridge here was built in 1797 and called the Falls Bridge for its proximity to the Little Falls of the Potomac. The second bridge here was built in 1808 and was suspended by iron chains anchored in stone abutments. The bridge then became known as Chain Bridge. The current bridge was built in 1938 and is the eighth one at this location.

Arlington Hall Junior College

The Arlington Hall School aimed to produce female graduates with a well-rounded emphasis on academics, physical education and the social graces. The school was opened in 1927 and closed in 1942 when the United States Government took it over to house the Army Signal Intelligence Service.

* ACPL-CFLH

A group of students at the fountain (around 1939).

Missionhurst-Lyonhurst

Missionhurst (formerly Lyonhurst) is currently owned by a Roman Catholic order, but it was built by Frank Lyon in 1907 as his home. Mr. Lyon was a prominent developer in the County and built many homes in the area now known as Lyon Park and Lyon Village. He also owned one of the first newspapers in the county, *The Chronicle*. His home was the first in the County to have electricity, using power brought from the railroad which ran down what is now Old Dominion Drive.

* ACPL-CFLH

Missionhurst

Cherrydale Elementary School (1919)

Students from the "new" Cherrydale Elementary School (1926)

BEST ALL AROUND

Virginia —
I guess I'll never
get the be days -over
back to Henry Clay.
rides rome with Sue
a will kinda
all remember
luck next year
as in the

Jo Schilling
Warren Beaty

Shelley Mann

Shep Morgan

MOST LIKELY TO SUCCEED

Washington Lee Yearbook (mid-1950's).

* Compliments of Virginia Palmer

Arlington County, Va.

*Most Rapidly Growing Part
of Greater Washington*

offers to the homeseeker quick
and convenient access to downtown Washington, with all of the
advantages of suburban life—
high elevation—fresh air—good
schools—good roads—natural
beauty.

No part of the county is more
than a few minutes' ride from
Washington in your own car, or
by bus or electric car.

Send for beautiful illustrated
booklet.

—◇❤◇—

**Arlington County
Chamber of Commerce**

Rucker Building
Clarendon, Va.

271

Arlington Farms

Arlington Farms provided temporary housing for women who worked in the government during World War II. The location is now part of Arlington National Cemetery.

* LOC

Intermission at one of the bi-weekly open house dances in the main lounge of Idaho Hall at Arlington Farms

* LOC

Sailors bicycle over to visit friends. While it existed, Arlington Farms was a popular place to visit for young men.

* ACPL-CFLH

Ready for work at the old Cherrydale Library, 1950's.

* LOC

The Milk Man-On Delivery

Ch. Ch. Ch. Ch. Changes... Same location, almost 100 years apart

The Church at Clarendon (1915).

The Church at Clarendon (1981).

The Church at Clarendon (2012).

Marymount University

Marymount opened in 1948 and was initially founded as a girl's high school. Arlington County granted an initial use permit for a high school for fifty young women ages 14 to 18. After one year, in 1949, an elementary school was added. In the fall of 1950 Marymount Junior College opened. Thirteen students enrolled the first year. In 1952 nine of the 13 initial students graduated. Bishop Ireton played a major role in the school's founding and expansion.

Currently Marymount enrolls more than 3,700 students representing approximately 40 states and 70 countries. Marymount is known for academic excellence, attention to the individual and a living and learning experience enriched by the resources of the nation's capital. Its programs combine a strong liberal arts foundation with solid career preparation; students in every major have opportunities to do original research, creative projects and exciting internships. Marymount has a proud and dedicated faculty with a student to teacher ratio of 13 to 1. Marymount University offers a learning environment that promotes student engagement and success.

Statue of Sister M. Majella Berg and two students in front of Caruthers Hall

The Old Rixey Mansion. The Main House at Marymount University.

The Arlington I have known

By State Senator Frank Ball

" *It is a great pleasure to know that people are interested in these old things. Arlington was a different Arlington then, completely different. It was made up of small farmers, a few government clerks, everybody raised something for the market to supplement his income. Nobody had any money after the Civil War. When I came along, everybody was just as poor as a church mouse. We were happy, had a good time. We children made our own playthings, our toys. If we got a 25cent present at Christmas, we thought we had a big Christmas. People were tight knitted together. We appreciated each other, we understood each other, families were more tightly knit. It was a very happy kind of living. This ridge (now Arlington Ridge Road) had no houses except the old congressman Campbell's house. It was so in the other parts of the County. Montgomery's manual of 1878 shows nearly every land holder in the County, approximately two or three hundred. The land was in the same names when I came along and I got to know nearly all of the families mentioned.*

Work was hard, money almost unknown, roads bad, schools primitive in equipment, law and order a minus at the bridgeheads, but family ties were close, community spirit warm and helpful, self-reliance outstanding and people had a good time.

Thank You for your kind attention to these few words about a long closed era. "

These words were spoken to a group at the Arlington Historical Society

May 8, 1964

For a more recent lighter view of Arlington check out

Arlington: The Rap by Remy Munasifi

available on YouTube "Go Remy" or on Itunes

Senator Frank L. Ball, *The Arlington I Have Known - The Arlington Historical Magazine*, 1964.

The Assassination of an American Nazi

George Rockwell was the founder of *"The American Nazi Party,"* which was based in Arlington. The presence of the party was an embarrassment to many Arlingtonians. Some never knew about it, or they ignored it. The group had made national headlines and had branches in several states, but was a nuisance more than anything. United States Attorney General Robert F. Kennedy declined to put the American Nazi Party on a list of dangerous domestic groups because he didn't want to boost their notoriety.

In the end the Party had an underwhelming legacy. It always seemed to be in shambles, moving its headquarters from house to house throughout Arlington. Rockwell was killed in the parking lot of the Dominion Hills Shopping Center off of Wilson Boulevard. Although Rockwell was despised by many it is ironic that is was a disgruntled former Nazi, who had risen to the number four slot in the hierarchy, who was arrested and convicted in the attack. The murder weapon was later found near Bluemont Park.

George Rockwell's lifeless body shortly after being shot and killed.

Shoot Out at Lee Harrison
Rival Gangs Clash-100 Shots Fired

On June 14, 1966 the rival gangs Pagans and Avengers were involved in a shootout at the Lee Harrison Shopping Center. Although police were tipped off in advance of the confrontation it still went on with a reported 100 shots fired. Police later impounded eight cars and confiscated dozens of weapons, including rifles, pistols, sawed-off shotguns and a baseball bat studded with nails.

Avengers:

The Arlington Gang. Mostly in their late teens and early 20's. Not afraid of a good fist fight but not "bad" in the world of gangs. At the time *"We were not a gang, just a bunch of guys hanging around Tops"* (the local drive-in located at the corner of Lee Highway and George Mason), recalled Wayne Hager.

Pagans:

The Pagans wanted to be *"bad"* and played their part. They were headquartered in Prince Georges County, Maryland. They aspired to be the East Coast branch of the Hells Angels. By the late 1960's and 1970's some Pagans would be linked to cases of torture, rape and murder.

How the clash started:

There were some common acquaintances between the gangs. Some members of each gang grew up together while others attended the same concerts and races. They hung out in the same circles. The shootout was arranged because of events that had happened the weekend before in North Beach, Maryland. A Pagan named Samuel Frederick was in a bar with some Avengers. Eventually tempers flared and Frederick was challenged to fight an Avenger named Rusty O'Brien. The fight was a draw with no serious injuries. As Frederick was riding his motorcycle back home, he crashed into the back of a truck and was killed. When Pagans heard the news they blamed the Avengers. Word spread to members of both gangs that Tuesday night at the *"lot,"* they would settle their differences.

Charles Clark, *Arlington's Night of Gang Warfare - Arlington Historical Society Magazine*, 2008.

Route 66 & Metro

The planning for Arlington began to change in the late 1950's and 1960's. The outlying suburbs of Falls Church, Fairfax, Manassas, Springfield and Loudoun County were growing. The County Board realized what this meant: the only way to commute to Washington, D.C. was through Arlington. At the same time the once thriving shopping district of Clarendon was beginning to lose its appeal and stores were leaving for the newer areas west.

The Board knew well in advance that they wanted to be part of The Metro system. This was the best way to move people through the County to Washington, D.C. as well as to support the County's shopping districts, add more dwellings, office space and night life.

What the state and Federal governments wanted were highways. It was a very real possibility that Arlington could have ended up similar to Los Angeles, with a much larger infrastructure of massive highways and bridges. There was Congressional support behind this; a National Highway Act had already been passed and of course the National Automobile Dealers Association was ready to supply big money to make this happen.

In the end, compromises were made. The County got Metro and the state government got its highway. But it was not easy. There was fierce opposition from local residents against the construction of Interstate 66. This was going to wipe out homes and neighborhoods throughout North Arlington. The original plan for I-66 had a spur road which would have ended up at a new massive bridge crossing at Three Sisters Islands. After 20 years of planning, opposition, and lawsuits, the construction of I-66 began. But I-66 was less than half the size of the original plan. The spur and additional bridge at Three Sisters Islands were not there. Trucks were not allowed. Instead of eight lanes of highway there were only four. A bike trail was added. The most sophisticated sound controls to date were added for the community as well as creative architectural design and vegetation plantings.

The Battle for Metro

"Battle" was the key word. Unfortunately the battle for Metro was happening at the same time as the opposition to Interstate 66. Metro had already been approved. Federal funding and bonds were set in place. The question now was *"Where will Metro go?"* The state and Federal Governments' decision was that Metro would follow I-66. This made sense. The land was already available. It was by far the fastest and least expensive way to complete

the project. For the state's and Federal government's purpose of moving people through Arlington, this was an ideal plan. But this plan did not work for Arlington. The County Board knew it needed additional stations along the Ballston to Rosslyn corridor. It needed the population growth and office space that these stations would bring. However, it was relying on Federal funding, so the issue was very delicate. In the end, through a long, persuasive, educational and ever- changing process, Arlington got what it wanted including an additional station at Virginia Square that was added at the 11th hour and was a real bonus for the County. Metro in Arlington is now seen as a great model of urban planning development. It must be *"Smart Growth."*

The Arlington Way:

The community and its citizens being involved in the planning and decision making in the County that affect their neighborhood, homes and growth.

* Photographer Greg Embree

Ballston Metro Station (2012).

Superdance
Bishop O'Connell High School

Superdance is a 12-hour dance marathon held annually at Bishop O'Connell High School to raise money for the Cystic Fibrosis Foundation. The event was started in 1975 by Principal Msgr. McMurtrie and student Maura O'Donnell whose sister had recently died from Cystic Fibrosis. Maura O'Donnell graduated from O'Connell and went on to nursing school but also died from Cystic Fibrosis. More than ninety five percent of the student body participate each year. The 12 hours are packed with live bands, DJ's, games and more.

In 2000, on the 25th Anniversary of Superdance, the event raised $197,500 to help find a cure for Cystic Fibrosis.

2001 was the highest grand total for any single year, raising $200,000.

The ten-year total from 2000 until 2010 was $1,837,326!!!!

Not Bad for a High School Fundraiser!!!!!

* Compliments of O'Connell High School

* Compliments of O'Connell High School

A Couple of
Arlington Spy Connections

Aldrich Ames

The McLean High School graduate, Arlington resident, and CIA counterintelligence officer was arrested and convicted of spying for the Soviet Union and Russia. Ames lived on North Randolph Street in Arlington. He was eventually caught by the free-spending life style he lived with his wife. Despite an annual salary of $60,000 Ames was able to afford a $50,000 Jaguar automobile, purchase his home for $540,000 in cash, and had monthly credit card bills that exceeded his monthly salary. It is unfortunate and almost hard to believe he was not caught sooner. The intelligence community was well aware that there were moles in the system compromising intelligence sources. Ames twice passed lie detector tests and said that it was his wife's family in Bogota, Columbia, which helped them financially. Ames secretly passed on highly sensitive information to informants which led to more than a dozen CIA operatives being executed by the Soviets. Ames pleaded guilty and is serving a sentence of life in prison. "You must have the wrong man!" Ames screamed as he was pulled over on North Quebec Street. They didn't have the wrong man; they finally had the right one.

Robert Hanssen

A former FBI agent who pleaded guilty to espionage is serving life in prison without possibility of parole. Hanssen was selling classified information to the Soviet Union-Russia for a period extending over 22 years, from 1979 to 2001. Possibly the worst spy of all time. Hanssen was married and had six children. A practicing Catholic, he attended mass regularly including the 6:30a.m. week day mass. In hindsight, it is not surprising that Hanssen lived a secret personal life along with his business life as a spy. At times he was a strip club regular and shared the most intimate details of his marriage on the internet and with a friend whom he would secretly let watch. For the FBI, Hanssen was one of the worst possible prospects to become a spy. He was brilliant on computers and had high level access to national security and intelligence secrets. Hanssen seemed to enjoy his part in the spy game, enjoying the secret relationship and being "thanked" for his services. One of Hanssen's "drop dead sites" was in Arlington along Long Branch Nature Preserve. Hanssen would never publicly meet his informants. Meetings would be arranged through a chalk or white tape marking of a predetermined public place such as a mailbox or sign. Days later secret information and payments would be made by taping the material to the bottom of a footpath or bridge, leaving it there for either party to recover. Hanssen was always the one to arrange the "drop dead sites" and refused when his informant suggested a site.

Arlington County Fire Department

The first county fire department was the Cherrydale Fire Department, which started in 1898 and was officially established in 1904. It originally consisted of 10 leather buckets, a ladder and spirited (or crazy) volunteers. A community fundraising effort, including a personal contribution from President Woodrow Wilson, resulted in the construction of the Cherrydale Firehouse which opened in 1919. Most early firehouses also acted as the local community center for all kinds of civic, social and fundraising activities.

Today the Arlington County Fire Department is among the best in the nation. It is regarded within the profession as an innovator and leader in enhancing fire service. Its 319 employees provide services through a combination of education, prevention and effective response to fire, medical and environmental emergencies.

Mission Statement:

We serve the Community with compassion, integrity, and commitment through prevention, education and a professional response to all hazards.

* ACPL-CFLH

Rescuing a fellow fire fighter from smoke inhalation (1962).

Arlington's first fire trucks

Clarendon Volunteer Fire Department-Hand Drawn Fire Fighting Wagon (1909).
Arlington's first fire fighting vehicle was a wagon that was dragged to fires by volunteer firemen.
Water was pumped out of nearby wells to fill the wagon's dozen buckets and, with luck, douse the flames.

A few years later. Ford truck with two 60 gallon mounted water tanks.
Clarendon Volunteer Fire Department. (Photo taken Jan 17, 1920 by James W. Tucker.)

Ballston Volunteer Fire Department, Company #2 (1923).

Clarendon Volunteer Fire Department. Night Squad (1931).

Clarendon Volunteer Fire Department

1947 Cadillac Ambulance, 1944 Chevrolet-Oren 500 GPM Pumper, 1949 Ward Le France 750 GPM Pumper,
1946 American La France 85 Foot Ariel Ladder

William D. Mackin
Taking the truck for a spin (Mid 1940's).

Cherrydale Fire Department with Sam Torrey Shoe Repair (Mid 1940's?).

Fire Station 4 (1982).

Arlington County Police Department

A DRINKING DRIVER
NEEDS
A POLICEMAN
FOR A CHASER

* ACPL-CFLH

Time to get tough!!!

* ACPL-CFLH

Practice makes perfect!!

Bicycle check, safety comes first

New Technology: Walk / Don't Walk

Arlington Crossing Guard

Safety time with student patrols. Possibly at St. Charles school

SCENIC ARLINGTON

Georgetown University from the George Washington Parkway.

A Fall day on the banks of the Potomac

Winter on the banks of the Potomac

Air Force Memorial unveiled October 14, 2006.

* Shutterstock.com

"To all who have climbed sunward and chased the shouting wind, America stops to say: your service and your sacrifice will be remembered forever, and honored in this place by the citizens of a free and grateful nation."
President George W. Bush

A classic view from Arlington:
Jefferson Memorial
Washington Monument
Capital Building

* Photographer Greg Embree

The Netherlands Carillon

* Photographer Greg Embree

"From the people of the Netherlands to the people of the United States in gratitude for assistance given during and after WWII"

A Springtime view of Rosslyn.

* Shutterstock.com

Sunset on the Potomac and the Three Sisters.

* Photographer Greg Embree

The old Jack's Boats, now the Key Bridge Boat House. Picture taken from Key Bridge.

Potomac Boat Club from the Arlington side of the River.

"Love" the Pink House on Washington Boulevard.

An old house with pride.

Sightseeing on the Potomac, 2013. View from the George Washington Parkway across to Washington, D.C.

The Navy and Marine Memorial dedicated to Americans Lost at Sea. Just off the George Washington Parkway across from the Pentagon.

An old Volkswagen on Four Mile Run

A quiet day on the river. Picture taken from Key Bridge.

* Photographer Greg Embree

The Kennedy Center- A classic site for all Arlingtonians and those who commute through Arlington into Washington, D.C.

The Washington Monument from Rosslyn.

Daffodils at dawn.

Marine Corps Memorial

In honor and memory of the men and women of the U.S. Marine Corps who have given their lives to their country since 10 November (1775).

Another shot of Georgetown University.

July 4, viewing the fireworks on the mall from Arlington.

One of the Westover Murals. This one is in the back parking lot and back entrance.
The mural artist are Britt Irick, Lane Bowen, Alex Bonefield and Wendy Daley.

Painting inside Whitlow's restaurant in Clarendon. The artist is Brian King who owns Artifice Inc. in Arlington.

IT'S JUST BUSINESS

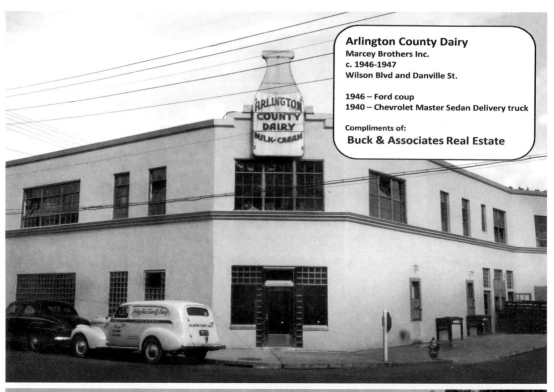

Arlington County Dairy
Marcey Brothers Inc.
c. 1946-1947
Wilson Blvd and Danville St.

1946 – Ford coup
1940 – Chevrolet Master Sedan Delivery truck

Compliments of:
Buck & Associates Real Estate

* ACPL-CFLH

Buckingham Theatre (early 1980's). The present day home of the U.S. Post office.

Cherrydale Cement Block Co. Inc. (1930's).

Virginia Hardware (1924).

Ellis Radio (1940's ?).

Bergmann's Laundry (1920).

* ACPL-CFLH

Cherrydale Drug Fair. The place for a malt or milk shake. Also was the site to several sit-ins during the time of racial segregation. On at least one occasion it was a peaceful event until Rockwell and his fellow Nazis showed up to stir trouble.

* ACPL-CFLH

Kirby's Esso Station, 1940's. Lee Highway near Irving Street.

Kann's Virginia

WELCOMES YOU TO A NEW ADVENTURE

IN SHOPPING CONVENIENCE

a good time to re-state

Kann's 58-year-old principle

"The customer is always right"

* Compliments of Bill Vogelson

Kann's was Arlington's main department store in the 1950's and 1960's.
Located at the corner of Washington Blvd. and N.Kirkwod. Did you see the live monkey in the children's shoe department?

Virginia Palmer, standing on the roof of the old J.C. Penney in Clarendon. * Compliments of Virginia Palmer
Virginia was doing research for her first job as Society Editor for the Sun Newspaper. (Late 1950's).

Opened in 1952 by Dr. Leonard Muse to serve African Americans during the time of racial segregation. This is a cherished business in South Arlington's Nauck neighborhood and in Arlington's history. In 2013 the Arlington County Board designated the Green Valley Pharmacy as the 33rd Arlington Historic District. Thank You to Dr. Muse for his perseverance, dedication, willingness to help others, believing in his business and community to make Arlington a better place.

Victory Bicycle Shop (1950's). 3136 North 10th Street.

* ACPL-CFLH

Rucker Lumber

* ACPL-CFLH

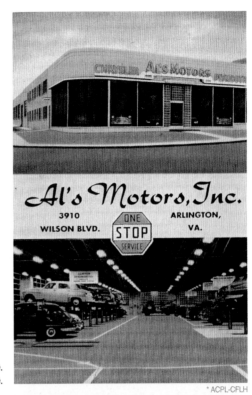

Even in the 1950's it's all about service.
Al's Motors One Stop Service.

Kenyon-Peck Service is our Business. This location is the current home to Walgreens in Clarendon.

Studebaker dealership with Amoco gas station (1950). Present day location of American Service Center.

The Hecht Company (1952), where Ballston Commons is today.

Now and then, The Broiler and Alcova Motor Company.
Same building on Columbia Pike.

The Broiler since 1970.

Alcova Motors (1920's)

Casual Adventure is another family owned and operated Arlington business. Originally started as a small grocery store by Oscar Stern in 1945, from 1955 to 1985 it became the Surplus Center. The business is now run by Oscar's grandson Neil, the store has evolved with the times. Casual Adventure is one of the leading outdoor stores in the metro area, with each season bringing in cutting edge products by the best manufacturers while providing the customer service of your neighborhood store.

"From Great Falls to Nepal" pretty much sums it up. Something for everyone.   casualadventure.com

Locally owned and operated. Cherrydale Hardware has been in business for more than 70 years. A snapshot of Arlington's past that is still a thriving business.

Preston's Now and Then

Located one mile west on Lee Highway from the original business.

The original store located at the corner of Glebe Road and Lee Highway.

Northern Virginia's oldest tattoo parlor. Rick was cool before tattoos were.

Owned by W&L graduate Wade Aylor and business partner Bill Pacheco. Wade and Bill worked together as mechanics for 20 plus years for Steve Craven at Craven Tire on Lee Highway before he sold his business and Wade and Bill moved on to open Cherrydale Motors.

A neighborhood store with a national reputation. Not just for wine, try the gourmet foods, cheeses, beer and spirits. Stop by for their tastings on Friday and Saturdays. A passionate staff encourages customers to learn, explore, enjoy and have fun.

Opened by John Ayers in 1947. Mr. Ayers was dedicated to his business and community and became known as the "Mayor of Westover." An old school neighborhood store that is still family run, with something for everyone.

Public Shoe Store has been offering shoes for the entire family since 1938. Located in downtown Clarendon they specialize in shoes and fittings for wide and hurting feet. Owner Dr. S.H. Friedman is committed to providing the best pair of shoes for each individual. Seventy-five years and counting.

One of the last neighborhood markets. In business for over 50 years, the market has its own butcher shop and offers more than 1,000 beers. Visit the beer garden for lunch or dinner. Part of the Best of Arlington.

Hurt Cleaners Now and Then

* ACPL-CFLH

Same location as the old Clarendon Station. Now the home of Northside Social.

Current location is one mile west on Wilson Blvd.

Most locals have a memory from the Cinema Drafthouse or the theatre. The "Drafthouse" replaced the Arlington Theatre also known as "Old Arlington" in 1985. The building itself is more than 70 years old and has a long history of providing entertainment. Still tucked behind the large movie screen is the original theatre stage equipped with lighting, storage and a green room. The theatre is owned and operated by a local family looking to continue the tradition of "Old Arlington."

La Maison is new in the neighborhood but already has a great reputation for special gifts.

Company Flowers and Gifts.
The best quality flowers delivered daily with a great design team to make beautiful arrangements for any occasion.
Also a full service gift shop for special gifts or small favors.

Bill's True Value Garden Center

Arlington's Markets and Grocery Stores.

ARLINGTON MARKET
BEER & WINE

SERVING THE COMMUNITY SINCE 1996

WHOLE FOODS MARKET

ARLINGTON

LA UNION GROCERY 703-812-9484

A few more in Arlington.

Hair Vogue for over 30 years in North Arlington.
Come visit Val the Greek God of Hair or Kosta the Greek God of Olive Oil.

Sun and Moon Yoga offering many types of classes and workshops promoting health and healing

Come and visit Chuck or Tom for framing and Sara Pitkin for custom designed jewelry.

Revolution Cycles.
Located in Clarendon.

Buckingham Center home to
Ravi Kabob and more.

Channel 7. Headquartered in Rosslyn.

PBS. Headquartered in Crystal City.

RESTAURANTS

The Little Tea House

Located on Arlington Ridge Road, the Little Tea House was a world famous gathering place of well knowns. One night it would have been possible to have seen diplomats or Amelia Earhardt, who would come up from nearby Hoover Airport. It has been said that more important world decisions were made at The Tea House than in Washington, D.C. It was built in 1920 and closed in 1963.

The
Little Tea House

ARLINGTON
Virginia

Make Reservations for Luncheon, Supper, or Special Parties
by Telephoning Jackson 1852

GERTRUDE LYNDE CROCKER

* ACPL-CFLH

Deviled crab with salad
Hot breads and beverage--75¢

PLATE LUNCHEONS
Including
HOT BREAD and BEVERAGES

GIBLETS WITH SHERRY SAUCE
SERVED ON TOAST POINTS 60¢

TOMATO FILLED WITH CRAB
FLAKE .... 75¢

FRESH SHRIMP SALAD IN
TOMATO ASPIC RING .... 75¢

SAUTED FRESH MUSHROOMS
WITH SALAD .... 75¢

SALAD BOWL OF VEGETABLES 60¢

SPAGHETTI AND HAM WITH
CREOLE SAUCE AND
SALAD .... 60¢

CHICKEN IN TIMBALE WITH
ONE VEGETABLE .... 90¢

CHEESE SOUFFLE' WITH
ONE VEGETABLE .... 90¢

HOT FRESH VEGETABLE
PLATE .... 90¢

BEEFSTEAK PIE WITH ONE
VEGETABLE .... 75¢

TOMATO STUFFED WITH
COTTAGE CHEESE .... 75¢

JELLIED FRUIT SALAD .... 75¢

(The above include choice
of one of following:
Tomato Cocktail, Fruit Cup,
Soup, Salad, Dessert)

THE
LITTLE TEA HOUSE

Served from 12 - 8:30 P. M.

CHOICE OF FRESH FRUIT CUP, TOMATO COCKTAIL, OR SOUP
VEGETABLES, HOT BREADS, BEVERAGES AND DESSERT

FILET MIGNON WITH FRESH BROILED MUSHROOMS -
Four Courses..................................$2.00

FRIED OR BROILED HALF SPRING CHICKEN -
Four Courses..................................$1.75
Three Courses.................................$1.50

TENDERLOIN STEAK -
Four Courses $1.50

CREAMED CHICKEN -
Four Courses $1.50

CHICKEN A LA KING -
Four Courses $1.50

CHICKEN SALAD -
Three Courses $1.50

BAKED HAM -
Three Courses $1.10

CHICKEN PIE -
Three Courses $1.10

COLD BAKED HAM WITH VEGETABLE SALAD $1.00

Don't you like our brown Bread? It's for sale at
20¢ a Pound

SANDWICH SUGGESTIONS

CHICKEN SANDWICH
WITH TEA OR COFFEE... 70¢

HAM SALAD SANDWICH
WITH TEA OR COFFEE... 40¢

CONSERVE TRAY AND SPOON
BREAD WITH ABOVE..... 25¢

SOUP TO ORDER ... 15¢ - 25¢

DESSERTS AND SALADS TO
ORDER WITH MEAL .... 20¢

(The Conserve Tray, including the Tea House Famous
Spoon Bread, is served
with Luncheon and Dinner).

* ACPL-CFLH

The original **Whitey's**

Photographer, Paula Endo - see page 4

Now the home to Eat Bar and Tallula.

In 1953, James J. Matthews opened Tops Drive Inn. It became an 18 unit restaurant chain in Arlington and the D.C. metro area. Matthews was a friend of Colonel Harlan Sanders, who founded Kentucky Fried Chicken. Mathews secured exclusive rights for serving the Colonel's recipe chicken and served on KFC's board after Colonel Sanders retired. If you Google Tops Drive Inn, you can view a 1957 tv commercial that was on the Milt Grant show.

Tops Drive Inn, Wilson Boulevard (1956).

The Queen Bee, one of my parents' favorite restaurants.

Recently closed Tom Sarris' Orleans House was a Rosslyn staple for many years.

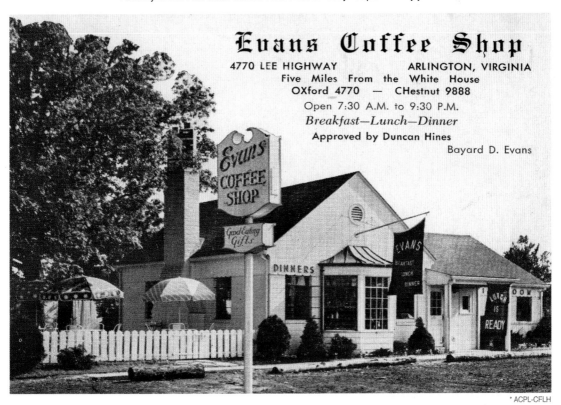

Evans Coffee Shop

4770 LEE HIGHWAY   ARLINGTON, VIRGINIA

Five Miles From the White House

OXford 4770 — CHestnut 9888

Open 7:30 A.M. to 9:30 P.M.

Breakfast—Lunch—Dinner

Approved by Duncan Hines

Bayard D. Evans

The Evans later opened Evans Farm Inn in McLean. Evans Coffee Shop later became The Alpine which recently closed.

Hot Shoppe's were a locally owned chain started by J.Willard Marriott in 1927. Marriott moved to the local area from Utah. Hot Shoppe's brand was built on two slogans: "food for the entire family" and "square meals at a fair price." Eventually Marriott's commitment to service and hospitality led to the first hotel. The Twin Bridges Motor Hotel opened in 1957 and was located near the 14th Street Bridge in Arlington. Marriott became a global brand in the hotel industry. By 1960, there were 70 Hot Shoppes in the local area and seven states. Famous jazz musician Duke Ellington and his band recorded seven versions of the Hot Shoppe's theme song, which aired in radio ads from 1967-1968.

Key Bridge Hot Shoppe (1949).

* ACPL-CFLH

* ACPL-CFLH

Fine Dining at the Rixey Mansion. Now the Main Hall at Marymount University.

Still operating in South Arlington. The Weenie Beenie was named after a famous pool player.

World's best pizza…after 2a.m.… Mario's is an Arlington landmark.

Arlington's original coffee house opened in 1996. Another locally owned neighborhood business in Arlington.
Part of the Clarendon-Court House community.

Greg and Susie Cahill re-opened the well-known D.C. restaurant Whitlow's in 1995 and re-named it Whitlow's on Wilson. They took over the old Town House Furniture Store. Whitlow's on Wilson was one of the first modern businesses to hit Clarendon and has helped make Clarendon the thriving neighborhood that it is today.

EL POLLO RICO
RESTAURANT & CARRY-OUT
POLLO A LA BRASA
Charcoal-Broiled Chicken

For many years….Arlington's best chicken. Pollo Rico.

Rays (aka Michael Landrum) took Arlington by storm serving great quality steaks. Another venture, Rays Hell Burger was a huge hit including a visit by President Obama. Rays is still going strong with 3 businesses in Arlington.

Live music forever at Iota Club and Café. Also open for breakfast, lunch and dinner.

An Arlington tradition in the Westover neighborhood since 1985, Lost Dog Café has recently expanded to open stores in South Arlington, McLean and Merrifield. Since 2001, Lost Dog and Cat and Rescue Foundation has saved the lives of more than 18,000 dogs and cats. A landmark business serving the community.

A Clarendon neighborhood favorite. Serving breakfast, lunch and dinner with a wine bar opening at 5p.m.

Another Arlington landmark business. When owner Wolfgang Buchler moved to the local area from Heidelburg, Germany, he couldn't speak English and never imagined he would be designing cakes for presidents. Since 1975 Wolfgang and wife Carla have been making great breads, pastries, deli foods and desserts. They are now making the wedding cakes for the children of couples who had their original cakes made by Heidelburg.   www.heidelbergbakery.com

A great mural for Rocklands on Washington Boulevard. Come back for their barbecue.

New Diner & Old Diner

The new Diner. Not that new anymore, opened in 1995. A New York style Diner-Restaurant with an on-site bakery. The results have been a great success of American favorites. Guy Fieri and his hit tv show, Diners-Drive Inns and Dives, visited Metro 29 and raved about the French Toast and Leg of Lamb.

The old diner. Old school diner that has been an Arlington business for more than 50 years.
Open 24 hours in classic diner style, Bob and Edith's is located on Columbia Pike in South Arlington.

* Photographer Greg Embree

Opened in 1986, The Carlyle Grand Café helped re-invent Shirlington after the shopping district had some lean years throughout the 1970's and early 1980's. Now known as "Carlyle" it has been the backbone of Shirlington for almost thirty years and is consistently a great restaurant.

Busboys and Poets, one of the newer additions to Shirlington.

Already an Arlington landmark. The Italian Store has been owned by the Tramonte family for more than thirty years. An Italian specialty shop known for great subs and NY pizza. Try the Milano. Also offering homemade pastas, sauces, unique wines, meats and cheeses.Truly a great Arlington business. Try their new location in Westover.

NBA Hall of Famer and original dream team member John Stockton making pizza at the Italian Store. The Italian pizza chef teaching John how to make pizza told owner Bob Tramonte, "He would be a good pizza chef." "Why" replied Bob, "because he has big hands." This makes sense; those hands are special making him the NBA's all-time assist leader with 15,806.

Pasha Café, the definition of a neighborhood restaurant. Since the 1990's serving Mediterranean fare in North Arlington.

Cowboy Café, a local watering hole on Lee Highway serving lunch and dinner with breakfast on weekends.

Tanios and Marie Abi-Najan along with their five children immigrated to the United States in 1976. In the middle of the night, the family boarded a cargo ship to escape the civil war in Lebanon. The final destination was Arlington, Virginia, where other family members were already living. By 1979 the family had saved enough to purchase a small restaurant in the Westover neighborhood where they lived. Being practical, they kept the original sign, "Athena Taverna," but changed one word, and Lebanese Taverna was born. Today Lebanese Taverna has six restaurants, four quick service cafes, a market and a full service catering division. Tanios and Marie have retired, and the five siblings each have a role in running the business.   lebanesetaverna.com

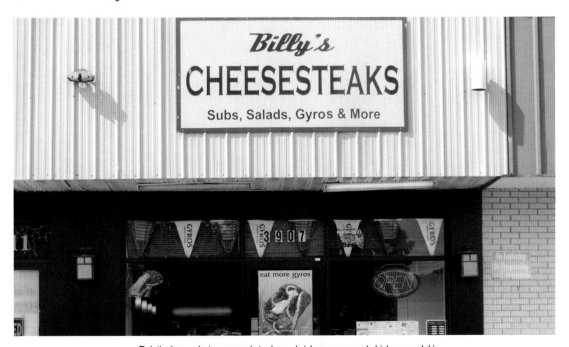

Relatively new but very good steak sandwiches, gyros and chicken souvlaki.

Part of local restaurant group, Great American Restaurants, Best Buns is well established in its Shirlington neighborhood.

A newcomer to Arlington. You have to try the pizza here.

Five Guys first restaurant was in Arlington, Virginia. In 1986, Jerry and Janie Murrell offered a proposal to their four sons. The oldest was getting close to attending college. They had a family meeting with a choice: "start a business or go to college." The business path won. The first Five Guys was take-out only. During the late 1980's and 1990's the Murrell family perfected their system. Four more Five Guys were opened. In 2003 they began offering franchise opportunities. In just over 18 months Five Guys Enterprises sold options for more than 300 units. Five Guys now has more than 1,000 stores open and another 1,500 committed to build. Not bad for a family take-out business started on Columbia Pike. fiveguys.com

Another locally owned family business with two locations in Arlington. Fresh, authentic and quality Mexican fare.

Where restaurant meets coffee shop. The first New Zealand-themed restaurant in Arlington.

Chili-Wings-Burgers-Sports
In October, 2005, *USA Today* named Hard Times as one of the ten best places in the country to have a bowl of chili.

Founded by three college friends. Crystal City Sports Pub is the driving force in their neighborhood.

A new classic bar!

An old classic bar!

The best of Crystal City by famed chef Jose Andres.

* Compliments of Gail Baker

Another family owned neighborhood restaurant. Used to be the home of Gifford's ice cream.

Started as a food truck... Now a thriving business in North Arlington.

A few more neighborhood favorites.

FAMOUS ARLINGTONIANS

Katie Couric

Katie Couric was born in Arlington, Virginia and attended Jamestown Elementary School, Williamsburg Middle School and Yorktown High School. Katie was a cheerleader while at Yorktown. After high school she attended the University of Virginia where she served in several positions for the school's award-winning daily newspaper, The Cavalier Daily and was a Delta Delta Delta Sorority sister. She graduated in 1979 with a bachelor's degree in English.

Early Career:

Katie's first job in 1979 was at the ABC News Bureau in Washington, D.C. Later she joined CNN as an assignment editor. In 1984 she left for Miami where she worked as a general assignment reporter for WTUJ. After a few years she returned to Washington to report for WRC-TV. During this time she won an Associated Press award and an Emmy.

Big Time:

In 1989 Katie joined NBC News as the Deputy Pentagon Correspondant and also was an anchor substitute at Today. She became a permanent co-anchor in 1991. She remained at Today for 15 years. In 2006 Katie moved to CBS to become the anchor and managing Editor of CBS Evening News. She became the first solo female anchor of the "big three" weekday nightly news broadcasts. In 2011 Katie returned to ABC to host a daytime talk show along with a long list of other responsibilities. In 2013 Katie was hired as the Global Anchor of Yahoo News.

THE INTERVIEWS:

Wow:

Over her career Katie has interviewed: Michelle Obama, Justin Bieber, Ellen DeGeneres, Bill Gates, Rahm Emmanual, Drew Brees, Sarah Palin, Chelsey Sullenberger, Valerie Plane, Robert Gates, Michelle Rhee, Barack Obama, Hillary Clinton, George W. Bush, Condoleezza Rice, John Edwards, Norah Jones, Michael J. Fox, Gerald Ford, Jimmy Carter, George HW Bush, Bill Clinton, Barbara Bush, John F. Kennedy Jr., Tony Blair, and JK Rowling. Just to name a few!!!

In her spare time she is also an author. Her first book, *The Best Advice I Ever Got: Lessons from Extraordinary* was a *New York Times* best seller.

To raise awareness of colon cancer Katie underwent a colonoscopy on-air in March 2000. She also was very active in the National Hockey League's Hockey Fights Cancer Campaign. She is currently a UNICEF Goodwill Ambassador for the United States. In 2005 Katie broadcast her own mammogram on the Today show as part of National Breast Cancer Awareness Month. As the guest of honor for the American Cancer Society Discovery Ball, she was recognized for her leadership in increasing cancer awareness and screening. In 2004 she was the honored guest at the 2004 Multiple Myeloma Research Foundation Fall Gala. In 2011 she became the Honorary National Chair of the National Parkinson's Foundation's Moving Day Campers. Now That's Impressive!!!!

Warren Beatty

Born in Richmond, Virginia, Warren moved to Arlington, Virginia, at an early age with his family. For many years his father was a school principal but turned to real estate as a new career a couple years after arriving in Arlington. While still a young child Warren became an avid reader. He was also a very talented piano player which he used for part time jobs while beginning his career. By the time Warren was entering Junior High he had a reputation for telling jokes and was a natural mimic, especially to one of his favorite comedians, Milton Berle. By the end of Junior High and entering Washington-Lee High School Warren became driven to make the school football team. He worked hard to become a star member of the team throughout high school. Warren had multiple scholarship offers to play football in college but did not accept any of them. He was also very involved in the Westover Baptist Church. The High School years were very successful for Warren. He had many friends, did very well academically, was involved in multiple school activities, the class President his senior year and ended up with the senior class superlative, "Best All Around."

After High School Warren attended Northwestern University. Before his sophomore year he moved to New York City and began to take acting classes. He did not return to college and never looked back. The career was just getting started. By this time Warren'solder sister and his closest companion as a child, Shirley MacLaine, was already a Hollywood star. Wanting to be a success on his own, Warren did not ask for help financially or through business contacts from both Shirley or his parents. There were times when he could have used the help while trying to support himself living in New York. But he was dedicated, focused and learning the ropes his own way. The smaller jobs started to come through and led to a bigger one. Warren was nominated for a Best Actor Tony Award for his performance in William Inge's drama, *A Loss of Roses*. It was his only show on Broadway. About this time Warren changed his last name from Beaty to Beatty.

The career then began to take off. He made his film debut opposite Natalie Wood in *Splendor in the Grass*, in 1961. Warren was nominated for a Golden Globe Award for his role. Then at age 29, Warren hit the Big One and they don't get much bigger. Warren produced and acted in *Bonnie and Clyde*, which was nominated for 10 Academy Awards including Best Actor for Warren. This film was an incredible success.

Warren is not just an actor. He is also a writer, producer and director. He wanted some control over his career. Other movies have been *McCabe & Mrs. Miller, the Parallax View, Shampoo, Heaven Can Wait, Ishtar, Reds, Bugsy* and *Dick Tracy*. The awards are too many to list. Warren is an icon, an innovator, and a legend who made and changed Hollywood.

Sandra Bullock

Sandra was born in Arlington, Virginia, but spent most of her early childhood years in Nuremberg, Germany. She studied ballet and vocal arts as a child. Sandra's mother was an opera singer and she frequently accompanied her mother on opera tours throughout Europe and sometimes took small parts in her mother's opera productions. Sandra returned to Arlington and attended Washington-Lee High School where she was a cheerleader and performed in high school theater productions. After graduating high school Sandra attended East Carolina University. After college Sandra moved to New York City to begin her career. While auditioning for roles she supported herself by bartending, waitressing and working as a coat checker. After a brief stay in New York Sandra was on her way to Los Angeles. The rest, as they say, is history.

WOW. I don't know where to start with this career which is still going strong. Sandra is an actress and producer who became famous in the early 90's. Some of her movies are *Demolition Man, Speed, A Time to Kill, The Net, Of Love and War, While You Were Sleeping, Miss Congeniality, Hope Floats, Two Weeks' Notice, Crash, The Proposal, The Blind Side, The Heat and Gravity*. Sandra was selected as one of *People* magazine's 50 most beautiful people in the world in 1996 and 1999. She also ranked 58th in *Empire* magazine's top Movie Stars of all Time. She was selected by *People* magazine as its "*Woman of the Year*" for 2010 and was ranked number 12 on *People's* most beautiful list 2011.

More than just an actress, Sandra runs her own production company, Fortis Films. She was executive producer of the *George Lopez* show. Fortis Films also produced *All About Steve*. Her father is the company CEO and her sister the former president. Sandra also opened a restaurant, Bess Bistro in Austin, Texas, and later opened another business, Walton's Fancy and Staple, which is a bakery, deli, upscale restaurant and floral shop. Sandra has been a supporter of the Red Cross on numerous occasions.

Shirley MacLaine

Shirley McLean Beaty was born in Richmond, Virginia, and moved to Arlington, Virginia before Junior High. She changed her name to Shirley MacLaine when she started her professional career. She was named after Shirley Temple. Both of her parents were educators. Shirley started taking ballet lessons as a young girl and continued with them through high school at the Washington School of Ballet. Attending the movies on Saturday afternoon with her younger brother Warren, was a regular event. At Washington-Lee High School Shirley was a cheerleader and acted in school drama productions. Between Junior and Senior year of high school, Shirley spent the summer in New York taking an intensive course at the School of American Ballet. After graduation, she moved to New York to act on Broadway where she was discovered by a film producer and signed to work for Paramount Pictures. Shirley later sued over this contract and is credited with ending the old-style studio star system of actor management.

The Career. This could be a book on its own but here is a glimpse. Shirley Maclaine's film debut began in 1955 in Alfred Hitchcock's *The Trouble with Harry*. Shirley won the Golden Globe Award for New Star of the Year – Actress. By 1959 Shirley was one of the most popular figures in the industry. *" She's the hottest properly in the business,"* according to hollywood experts. *"And off screen, she's the hottest conversation piece - no one as different as Shirley has come to town in years."* Other early movies were *Hot Spell, Around the World in Eighty Days, The Apartments, The Children's Hour,* and *Irma la Douce*. In 1978, Shirley was awarded the Women in Film Crystal Award. In 1983, she won an Oscar for her role in *Terms of Endearment*. In 1988, she won a Golden Globe for Best Actress for *Madame Sousatzka*. It seems like Shirley has worked with every star in Hollywood including Julia Roberts, Jack Lemmon, Elizabeth Taylor, Audrey Hepburn, Clint Eastwood, Anne Bancroft, Anthony Hopkins, Jack Nicholson, Meryl Streep, Kathy Bates, Nicholas Cage, Ricki Lake, Kevin Costner, Jennifer Aniston and Joan Collins to name just a few. In 2012, Shirley received the 40th AFI Life Achievement Award by the American Film Institute. In 2013, she received the Kennedy Center Honors for lifetime contributions to American culture through the performing arts.

In addition to her Hollywood career, Shirley is also an author and well known for her beliefs in new age spirituality and reincarnation. Several of her best-selling books are based on her spiritual beliefs as well as her Hollywood career. Legendary!!

Harris, Eleanor. *Shirley MacLaine - Hollywood's Free Spirit, Look Magazine*: September, 1959.

Tipper Gore

The former second lady of the United States. Mary Elizabeth Aitcheson was born in Washington, D.C., grew up in Arlington, Virginia, and attended St. Agnes High School in Alexandria. "Tipper" was a nickname given to her by her mother as a young girl. While in high school she played drums for a band, The Wildcats. She still has the drum set.

Tipper graduated from Boston University in 1970 and a few years later received a master's degree in psychology. She is the mother to four children and a proud grandmother. Tipper had a significant role as a successful politician's wife. She was very successful in her own causes to help make a difference. President Clinton appointed her as his official mental health advisor. She is a well-known speaker about depression from her own life's experiences.

Tipper has been an avid photographer for most of her adult life. It was a common sight for her to have her own camera at political events. Her camera is part of how she communicates the real story, preserving history and showing real life. She has published her own photography as well as being an author of several books.

Tom Dolan

From a young child swimming at Washington Golf and Country Club to back-to-back Gold Medalist in the 1996 and 2000 Olympic Games, Tom has enjoyed tremendous success in the pool. Tom was also a Silver medalist in the 2000 Olympics. He held the 400 individual medley record for nine years. Tom also won two Gold Medals at the World Championships and helped lead the University of Michigan to an NCAA team title in 1995. Tom was also a 14-time U.S. National Champion and was on the cover of *Sports Illustrated* and the *Wheaties* cereal box. He was also inducted into the International Swimming Hall of Fame. Not bad going from his early days of learning how to swim in Arlington, Virginia, to being one of the best all-around swimmers in the history of the sport.

Tom Dolan Swim School

From his experiences of swimming around the world Tom has opened a state-of-the-art purpose-built swim school facility and system that teaches swimmers solid fundamentals that are essential for water safety and recreational and competitive swimming. "Swim Thru Life" is the school's tag line, to provide water-safety education, self-esteem and confidence in the water, with safety skills and life lessons that will stay with kids forever.

ARLINGTON, VIRGINIA, DID YOU KNOW?

Key Bridge

The Key Bridge was built in 1923 to replace the Old Aqueduct Bridge crossing the Potomac from Rosslyn into Georgetown. The bridge was named in honor of the author of the "Star Spangled Banner" Francis Scott Key. He was a local attorney living very close to the bridge which now bears his name.

Old Dominion Drive

Named after the Great Falls & Old Dominion Railroad Line which ran from Rosslyn to Great Falls. In 1935 the line was abandoned and taken over by Arlington and Fairfax Counties for unpaid taxes.

Powhatan

The street and spring are named after the powerful Indian Chief who was the Father of Pocahontas.

Arlington Cemetery

Occupies just over half of the 1,100 acres of the original Arlington Plantation. The cemetery also has more than four million visitors each year.

Arlington House

Was built by George Washington Parke Custis and his slaves between 1802 and 1818.

Mary Custis Lee

Was courted by several young men, including a congressman from Tennessee named Sam Houston. Her heart was set on Robert E. Lee and they married in the family parlor at Arlington House on June 30, 1831.

Slaves at Arlington House

There were as many as 63 slaves who lived and worked at the Arlington House. All the slaves were freed on December 29, 1862, by the will of George Washington Parke Custis.

Lee Boys

The three sons of Robert E. Lee and Mary Custis Lee each served in the Confederate Army during the Civil War. All three survived the war. The three boys, Custis, Rooney and Rob Jr., shared one room while growing up at Arlington House.

William "Rooney" Lee

Joined the Confederate Army in 1861 and served under Jeb Stuart as a cavalry officer. Rooney was captured by Union troops at his wife's family home while recovering from a battle wound. He spent eight months as a prisoner of war before returning to the Confederate Army in an exchange.

Silent Movie Star Pola Negri

Local legend has it that Pola rented a house off of Military Road (now the Gulf Branch Nature Center) as a vacation house in the early 1930's. Her Virginia hideaway. Pola was one of the most popular stars of the silent movie era (1920's) who lived the Hollywood lifestyle including romances with Charlie Chaplin and Rudolph Valentino.

Jimmy Dean

The sausage king and country music star Jimmy Dean bought his first home in Arlington on North Roosevelt Street. He had his first radio job in Arlington at WARL, located at the corner of Lee Highway and North George Mason Drive. Dean also started his first TV show while living in Arlington. In 1958 Dean's contract was bought out by CBS to do a daily show in New York and the family moved to Connecticut.

Presidents at Arlington National Cemetery

There are only two Presidents buried in Arlington National Cemetery, John F. Kennedy and William Howard Taft.

Robert F. Kennedy

Out of more than 400,000, the funeral of Robert F. Kennedy is the only one to have taken place at night at Arlington National Cemetery.

Lt. Thomas Selfridge

Orville Wright's passenger on the flight that crashed on Sept. 17, 1908, at Fort Myer in Arlington became the first victim of an airplane crash.

Pentagon

The Pentagon was originally named the "War Department Building."

Arlington County Fire Department

In 1974 the Arlington County Fire Department hired the first professional female fire fighters in the nation.

RixeyMansion

In 1929 the German Embassy was located in the Rixey Mansion.

John Glenn

In 1962 Arlington resident John Glenn became the first American to orbit the earth, aboard Friendship 7.

BIBLIOGRAPHY

Arlington Historical Society. *Images of America-Arlington.* Arcadia: 2000

Berg, Sister M. Majella. *College to University: A Memoir.* Marymount University: Arlington, VA: 1999

Blount, Ray, Jr. *Robert E. Lee A Life.* Penguin Group: 2003

Dietrich, Zula. *Zula Remembers – South Arlington in Earlier Times.* Loft Press: 2005

Dodge, George W. *Images of America-Arlington National Cemetery.* Arcadia: 2006

Embree, Greg. *Maywood at a Milestone-A Centennial Snapshot,* 1909-2009. 2009

Finstad, Suzanne. *Warren Beatty- A Private Man.* Harmony Books: 2005

Gilmore, Matthew. *Historical Photos of Arlington County.* Turner: 2007

Gilmore, Matthew. *Remembering Arlington.* Turner: 2000

Goldberg, Alfred. *The Pentagon-The First Fifty Years.* Historical Office, Office of the Secretary of Defense, Washington, D.C.: 1992

Holt, Kathryn. *Cherrydale-Cherries, Characters and Characteristics.* 1986

Klein, Edward. *Katie-The Real Story.* Cravin Publishers: 2007

Knudsen, Robert G. *A Living Treasure-Seasonal Photographs of Arlington National Cemetery.* Potomac Books, Inc.: 2008

MacLaine, Shirley. My Lucky Stars-A Hollywood Memoir. Bantom Books: 1995

National Geographic. *Where Valor Rests-Arlington National Cemetery.*

Netherton, Nan and Ross. *Arlington County in Virginia: A Pictorial History.* The Dunning Company: 1987

Parzych, Cynthia. *Arlington National Cemetery-A Guided Tour through History.* Morris Books: 2009

Peters, James Edward. *Arlington National Cemetery-Shine to America's Heroes.* Woodbine House: 2008

Poole, Robert M. *On Hallowed Ground-The Story of Arlington National Cemetery.* Walker & Company: 2009

Pratt, Sherman. *Arlington County, Virginia, A Modern History.* Sherman Pratt-Book Crafters: 1997

Rose, C.B. Jr. *Arlington County, Virginia: A History.* Port City Press: 1976

Templeton, Eleanor Lee. *Arlington Heritage.* Avenel Books: 1959

Templeton, Eleanor Lee & Netherton, Nan. *Northern Virginia Heritage. Avenel Books:* 1959

Trudeau, Noah Andre. *Robert E. Lee.* Palgrave MacMillan: 2009

Vise, David A. *The Bureau and the Mole.* Atlantic Monthly Press: 2002

Weiner, Tim- Johnston, David-Lewis, Neil A. *Betrayal-The Story of Aldrich Ames, An American Spy.* Random House: 1995

The Arlington Historical Magazine, The Arlington Historical Society;

Ball, Senator Frank L. *The Arlington I Have Known*. 1964

Clark, Charles: *Arlington's Night of Gang Warfare*, 2008

Clark, Charles: *Orville Wright in Arlington*, 2008

Clark, Charles: *The Assassination of an Arlington Nazi*, 2005

Clark, Charles: *Jimmy Dean in Arlington*, 2009

Crane, Jennifer Sale: *Pola Negri Slept Here*, 2009

Doptis, Jean S: *Presley MarionRixey*, 1996

Fearson, Jim: *Chain Bridge*, 1991

Newman, Robert: *Eighty Years in a Sears Mail Order House*, 1987

Webb, Willard: *John W. Ayers: The Mayor of Westover*, 2010

Webb, Willard: *Mary Ann Hall: Arlington's Illustrious Madam*, 2004

Magazines and Other Publications

Arlington County Fire Department Historical Society, Arlington County Fire and Rescue Association, Arlington County Fire Department *"The Red Book" A Century of Service, The Fire and Rescue Service in Arlington County, Virginia*, Second Edition 2002, By Vinny Del Giodice, Editor, Arlington Fire Journal

Arlington Magazine. *Before Our Time-Special History Issue*: November/December 2013

Gordon, Meryl. *Tipper Gore 5 Years Later-More*: March 2006

Harris, Eleanor. *Shirley MacLaine - Hollywood's Free Spirit, Look Magazine*: September, 1959.

Historic Arlington, the Arlington County Bicentennial Celebration Task Force

Marymount University Main House (Rixey Mansion), 1976 Bicentennial

McElwaine, Sandra. *Tipper Gore: Smart! Fun! And a Fighter for Mom and Family-Good Housekeeping*: March, 1993

Marvullo, Joe. *What Tipper Sees-George*: August, 1998

National Geographic. *Special Edition-The Civil War, The Conflict That Changed America*: Summer, 2013

O'Leary, Frank. *The Greatest Scandal in Arlington History… The Saga of E. Wade Ball*

Spike, Paul. *Box-office Goddess-Vogue*: October, 1996

Sullivan, Robert. *Sandy gets serious-Vogue*: October, 2006